THE ORGANIZATION MAP

ABOUT THE AUTHOR

Pam McClellan's interest in organization was born from a desire to spend less time on house-related work and more time pursuing her personal interests. With that motivation, she began devising and investigating techniques, systems and shortcuts that would help her get and stay organized. Her personal success led to her own consulting business, helping homemakers and businesspeople simplify their lives. Through newspaper, television, and seminar appearances, Pam has brought her message, "Get organized and get on with your life!" to thousands. She and her family live near Nashville, Tennessee.

THE ORGANIZATION MAP

PAM McCLELLAN

BETTERWAY BOOKS
CINCINNATI, OHIO

Printed and bound in the United States of America.

97   96   95   94   93   5   4   3   2   1

Library of Congress Cataloging-in-Publication Data

McClellan, Pam.
   The organization map / by Pam McClellan.
     p.   cm.
  Includes index.
  ISBN 1-55870-316-0 (pbk.)
  1. Home economics. 2. Time management. I. Title.
TX301.M38   1993
640'.43 — dc20
                                                  93-28254
                                                   CIP

Designed by Sandy Conopeotis
Cover illustration by Sandy Conopeotis
Part and Chapter Opener illustrations by Magno Relojo, Jr.
Other illustrations by Jim Benton

*I*N MY LIFE, I HAVE HAD THE PRIVILEGE

TO KNOW SOME ORDINARY PEOPLE WITH SOME

EXTRAORDINARY POTENTIAL. SADLY, THEIR

POTENTIAL AND TALENTS LAY DORMANT

BECAUSE THEY'VE GOTTEN SIDETRACKED BY

THEIR OWN DISARRAY. THIS BOOK IS DEDICATED

TO THESE AND TO ALL THE OTHER ORDINARY

PEOPLE WITH SO MUCH TO OFFER A NEEDY

WORLD. PLEASE, DO US A FAVOR. GET GOING

AND GET ORGANIZED. WE NEED YOU!

ACKNOWLEDGMENTS

Thanks to Earline Phipps, Betty Bender and Helen Draschil, who gave me my first chance.

Thanks to Barb Schuetz and Jim Robertson of the *Columbia Daily Tribune* for giving me my own column.

Thanks to Bill Brohaugh at Betterway Books for being on my side.

And thanks to Steve and Keegan, who are my inspiration.

INTRODUCTION

So, you want to get organized? Well, it's about time. But what does being organized mean to you? If your goal is a home that is immaculate at all times, spotless children living in sanitized rooms, and a gourmet dinner for forty tucked away in the freezer "just in case," I have a word of advice: Get a life! There's nothing wrong with wanting to be comfortable, but being a slave to your home is not the answer. Besides, you can't have any fun in life if you are always worried about messing up the house.

If being perfect is out, what is fair to expect from yourself? Well, for most households the two biggest tasks are meal preparation and laundry. Everyone wants to eat and most of us prefer our clothes clean. Other tasks are more subjective. Technically, beds can go unmade, dusting can be put off, and the bathrooms can go unscrubbed. (Of course, if you are already living in a dusty house with unmade beds and dirty bathrooms, that's probably why you bought this book.) The point is, you need to decide what is important to you and your family (if you have one) during this stage of your life. Just as the seasons come and go, your needs will change as your life makes its natural progression.

When I decided to get organized, I did so predominantly for two reasons. The first was simple order. I wanted to be able to find what I needed when I needed it. I just didn't have an extra ten minutes to search for car keys. Even if I were to live forever, I wouldn't want to lose those ten minutes for such a ridiculous reason.

My second reason for getting organized was the realization that I had been wasting too much time on basic home maintenance. The way I had set up my house created mountains of unnecessary work. I was spending far too much time dusting and polishing, and I decided I'd rather live my life than clean it away. (I once calculated that there were approximately a zillion things I'd rather do than housework.) Since I like things clean and tidy (and I wasn't expecting a maid to show up and volunteer her services) I knew I had to find a way to make things easier and less time-consuming for myself.

It took a while, but through trial and error, I cut out the clutter, rearranged closets and drawers, established systems, got my paperwork under control and, in the process, simplified my life.

People have different ideas about what it means to get organized. Some people see getting organized as a cleanliness issue, while others view it merely as a way of maintaining sanity. Still others, and I am one, are motivated by the concept that a well-organized life gives us more free time to pursue matters of *real* interest. Whatever your motivation, it's a good idea to give some thought to the specific areas you want to improve.

If you are interested in revamping your entire home and lifestyle, simply follow the chapters and work through each room step by step. If you are particularly concerned about a specific area of your home, just skip ahead to that chapter. If you decide to skip around, please be sure to read chapters one through five first.

Whether you are concerned about getting a decent meal on the table each night or keeping up with the piles of laundry you are constantly battling, you should recognize that getting control over these things is your *goal*. Goal setting is an important concept to understand, because once you have established a reasonable goal, you can take steps to make it a *reality*. By carrying through with your plan one step at a time, you will be able to reach your final destination — an organized home.

I won the war over disarray, and now I want to help you wage your own battle. I'll take you through your home room by room, step by step, guiding you all the way. You'll learn how to manage time, identify clutter (and know what to do with it), organize closets and cabinets, file paperwork, and more. In doing so, you'll make your house a more pleasant place to live and work. You are on your way to a better life. Good luck!

PART ONE

LAYING YOUR FOUNDATION

SETTING GOALS AND GETTING STARTED

CHAPTER ONE

DECIDING HOW TO SPEND YOUR TIME

HOW TO RECAPTURE VALUABLE TIME

BY COMBINING TIME MANAGEMENT

WITH HOME MANAGEMENT SO THAT

YOU'LL NO LONGER BE A SLAVE

TO YOUR HOME

*I*f only I had more time!" Does that sound familiar? I must admit that the thought has crossed my mind a time or two. Unfortunately, we're stuck with twenty-four measly hours per day. The good news is: We all have exactly the same amount of time. So, why is it that some people accomplish so much while others accomplish so little? Are the "doers" sleeping less? Skipping meals? How do they get so much done?

The one common thread among people who are getting things done is successful time management skills. They understand that *time* is *life*. They know their time will be *spent* one way or another, so they've learned to get the best return on their investment. Those who lack basic time management skills are left frustrated and unful-filled, wondering why they can't seem to get anything done. It's not that they necessarily lack talent or energy. They lack direction. As someone once said: "They don't plan to fail; they fail to plan."

To be an effective organizer, you must utilize the proper organizing tools. One such tool is a solid time management plan. Successful people of all professions operate by using time management sched-ules. Let's consider doctors and dentists, for example. Except for an emergency, these people know, sometimes weeks in advance, who will be their patients and at what hour they can expect them. A dentist can't have people casually strolling in and out of her office at all hours of the day arbitrarily demanding root canals and X-rays. She can't put up with a receptionist whose idea of a work ethic is, "I'll show up when I feel like it." To be successful, she must operate her business with some sense of order, and with the cooperation of her patients and employees. You don't expect your dentist to operate under chaotic circumstances, and since you're a professional, too, you must operate like one.

There is no need to be intimidated by the concept of time manage-ment. Simply stated, all it means is you must make conscious deci-sions about how you will *spend* your time if you don't want to wind up *killing* it. After all, it's the most valuable, nonrenewable resource you have. You need to manage it wisely.

FINDING OUT WHERE YOUR TIME GOES — AN OPTIONAL EXERCISE

There are people who take on so many responsibilities that all their time is spoken for. On the other hand, when some people say, "I have no time," what they really mean is they have no time manage-ment skills. They sleep twelve hours a day, spend an hour doing their hair, and while away the afternoon watching Lucy and Ethel getting into trouble for the tenth time. They are not really lacking time, they are lacking solid time management.

If you have been wondering where your time goes, find out. Fill in the chart below, listing the time you think it takes to get various tasks accomplished. Add other things you do on a daily basis on the lines provided. As soon as you complete a task, write down the actual time spent. Don't wait until the end of the day to record your findings; it's too easy to forget.

As an example, you may think you watch TV only one hour a day. The reality may be that you keep it on all day for company, get distracted by it, and spend four or five hours, all told, watching. You may think it just takes five minutes to shower and ten minutes to put on makeup. The reality may be that you spend twenty minutes showering and another twenty minutes on makeup and hair. These examples aren't meant as accusations. I know how easy it is to lose track of time. The point is you want to identify how you spend your time so you can exercise maximum control over it.

Though this may be tedious, it can prove very enlightening if you have been frustrated about your lack of time.

I recommend you keep with you the chart below for at least three days so that you can see a pattern. Don't be ashamed of the truth. This is for your eyes only, and a true perspective is necessary for your own benefit.

Where My Time Goes

	ESTIMATED TIME	ACTUAL TIME Day 1	Day 2	Day 3
Sleeping	8			
Grooming	1			
Working (outside home)	9			
Travel time (to/from work)	1/2			
Meal prep and clean up	1			
Housework	1			
Hobbies	0			
Shopping	1/2			
Watching TV	3			
Exercising				

DOING TIME — EXERCISES FOR TIME MANAGEMENT

Similarly, you should find out how much time getting organized takes. Aside from the fact that housework isn't exactly a day at the beach, some people may struggle with it because they have the perception that some jobs are too time-consuming to be bothered with. Do you find yourself avoiding tasks because you don't want to take the time to do them? If so, I suggest you find out how long it actually takes to get a given task accomplished.

For instance, perhaps you never make your bed because it takes too long. A disability aside, it shouldn't take more than a few minutes. If you're spending ten minutes making a bed, something is wrong. Perhaps you're fussing with too many unnecessary things. A dust ruffle, for example, tends to slow the process by getting caught under the mattress when you are tucking in sheets. Also, positioning your bed so one side is against the wall can drive you crazy and make you want to skip the job. In this case, you can position the bed so that neither side is next to the wall and eliminate the dust ruffle by switching from a comforter to a bedspread. These two simple changes will make the job quicker and therefore more palatable.

When you pinpoint the things that cause work, but don't necessarily add to your pleasure, you can fix them. Think about this each time you resist or put off doing a housekeeping chore. Figure out how you can simplify tasks so that you are more willing to get them done.

TIME MANAGEMENT AND HOME MANAGEMENT

For our purposes, we will concentrate on time management in relation to organizing and maintaining the home. Aside from your organizing projects, there's still the basic household maintenance to be concerned with. You'll need to keep up on laundry, meal preparations, etc. Therefore, your first order of business is to organize your time. To do so, you will create a schedule for all the household jobs that need to be done on a regular basis. By doing this, you will know what will be done and when, just like our dentist friend.

One reason I think it's a good idea to schedule these jobs is because if we simply waited until we felt like doing them, we'd probably all be living in squalor. (I can't ever remember waking up and thinking, *What a beautiful day, I can't wait to scrub toilets! Fa la la.*) Once we determine what jobs need to be done on a regular basis, we can set out a plan for accomplishing that goal. Since they are going to have to be done sometime, you may as well exercise some control as to when. That's time management.

Let's face it, there are plenty of boring, mundane and downright yucky jobs associated with housework, but we still have to do them. Fortunately, most of us are motivated to get through these unpleasant tasks with the understanding that the end result is a worthy goal. Unless you can persuade (or pay) someone else to do your housework, you may as well map out a plan and learn techniques to make the best of the situation.

My advice for time management is this: Invest a relatively small amount of time in planning and strategy to gain a substantial return in time *well spent*.

CREATING A HOUSEHOLD WORK SCHEDULE

Your objective is to create a schedule for all the cleaning and household jobs that need to be done on a regular (but not daily) basis. This schedule repeats weekly. These jobs include:

- laundry
- vacuuming
- ironing
- bill paying, paperwork
- mending
- changing bed linens
- grocery shopping
- dusting
- scrubbing bathrooms
- organizing projects
- mopping floors

MY SCHEDULE

You will notice when you look at the sample of my weekly schedule (on page 12) that I do heavy cleaning only two days a week. I like the house to be in tip-top shape at the start of the week to get us off on the right foot. I also like it to be clean for the weekend so that it is pleasant when we are all home and able to enjoy each other's company. With that in mind, I scheduled Mondays and Thursdays as my two heavy cleaning days.

Monday I do laundry, vacuum, scrub the bathrooms, mop, dust and polish, as needed.

Tuesday is office day. I do paper-related tasks such as paying bills, writing letters and filing. It is also my telephoning day. If a call is not a "must do," I save it until Tuesday and group several together.

Wednesday is grocery day. I wipe down the fridge, finalize my shopping list, and do the weekly grocery shopping.

Thursday is my second heavy cleaning day of the week. I do the same things as on Monday (except mop). It goes quickly, because things are still in pretty good shape from Monday.

Friday I take off, except for daily work such as cooking and cleanup.

These are all household jobs that need to be done regularly, regardless of your age or gender. It's what I call "the everyday business of life." Because I have a plan for getting things done, I can relax. I needn't spend a moment worrying about when I will "get the chance" to do my grocery shopping or how I will "find the time" to clean our clothes. Scheduling also ensures that things won't get out of hand if something comes up. If for some reason I don't get my cleaning done on Monday, I know that I will get to it on Thursday.

For my own convenience, I arranged my schedule so these jobs can easily be completed by 10:30 A.M. That means I have the rest of the day to do as I please. For me, that includes my consulting business and my writing. By following my schedule, I have the best of both worlds. I am able to get my housework taken care of and still have time to pursue other interests.

Step One

Using a pencil, fill in your work schedule on the sample provided. If it's helpful, answer the questions below to assist your decision making.

1. Do you prefer getting the heavy cleaning done all at once or doing a little each day throughout the week?
2. Do you have any help available? Can you schedule it at a time that is convenient for you?
3. Are you a morning person or do you have more energy later in the day? Can you schedule your most demanding jobs accordingly?

Tips

- If you decide to schedule your jobs during afternoon or evening hours, I suggest you put a cap on the completion time. For instance, break the day into its three natural segments. Try to finish morning jobs before lunch, afternoon jobs before dinner and evening jobs before 10:00 P.M. Putting a cap on the time helps you keep the end in sight and may discourage you from stringing out your chores over the entire day.

- For a while, schedule your organizing projects, too. That way, you know you will have time for them. Eventually, your home will reach the level of organization you desire and you will simply need to maintain it.

- When preparing your schedule, be sure to block in time to pursue fun things that interest you. It may be easier to get through the work when you know you have something to look forward to.

You must develop a comfortable system, if you are going to be able to maintain it. Therefore, if necessary, rework your schedule until you are satisfied. (That's why you are using pencil!)

Step Two — Using a Daily "To Do" List

In addition to following a weekly work schedule, I suggest you use a daily "to do" list to help stay organized. Every well-organized person I know uses a daily to do list. Since some people are put off by lists, here are a few reasons why using one is helpful.

- Writing down your plans relieves you of the unnecessary burden of trying to remember everything you want to do. You won't have to go through the "I've got to remember to do such and such" and "Oh, I almost forgot to do so and so" routines.

- A list can help keep you focused, particularly if you are easily sidetracked. A momentary interruption won't throw you off, as long as you refer back to your list.

- I think having a list tends to keep your momentum going. As you cross off things you have accomplished, it may inspire you to finish up the other tasks.

- Your to do list, as well as your weekly work schedule, can help you pinpoint how you are spending your time. This is a valuable tool when you want to reassess your priorities.

	MONDAY	TUESDAY	WEDNESDAY	THURSDAY	FRIDAY	SATURDAY	SUNDAY
Morning	MORNING DAILIES laundry scrub bath(s) mop floors dust + polish vacuum **10:30 A.M.**	MORNING DAILIES office hour phone calls pay bills write letters	MORNING DAILIES clean refrigerator grocery shopping	MORNING DAILIES laundry scrub bath(s) dust vacuum	MORNING DAILIES off the rest of the day	MORNING DAILIES	OFF!
Afternoon	Afternoon time is available for work other than housework and/or other interests						
Evening	PM DAILIES (clean up after dinner) dinner Pick up	dinner PM DAILIES Pick up	Leftovers PM DAILIES Pick up	dinner PM DAILIES Pick up	FUN night PM DAILIES Pick up	dinner PM DAILIES Pick up	

	MONDAY	TUESDAY	WEDNESDAY	THURSDAY	FRIDAY	SATURDAY	SUNDAY
Morning							
Afternoon							
Evening							

- My personal favorite reason for keeping a list is the tremendous satisfaction of accomplishing a task and crossing it off!

When I first started using a to do list, I included the most routine things such as "get up," just so I could have the pleasure of crossing them off. What a nut. (I don't suggest you do that.) The things you should put on your to do list are the things you want to accomplish that are unique to the day: the doctor's appointment, having the car repaired, and shopping for a birthday present, for example. These things are in addition to your daily work and weekly work schedules. If this is new to you, I suggest you list a maximum of six items on your to do list. I caution you to avoid setting yourself up for failure by listing twenty-five things. As you get the hang of using this list, you will have a better understanding of what you can reasonably accomplish.

Set a specific time each evening to make your list, and do it consistently at that time. I have found that after dinner, when the kitchen has been cleaned, is a good time for me. I recommend doing the list in the evening, because it's usually a little less hectic than the morning. Also, you can drift off to sleep peacefully, without waking up and thinking, "I've got to remember to do such and such tomorrow." When you wake up in the morning, no time is wasted. Your list is prepared and you are ready to go.

By the way, if you are the type of person who has trouble getting motivated, start by tackling one of the more pleasant tasks on your list. On the other hand, if you are the type who needs a reason to get through the less pleasant tasks, save the fun ones for last.

ROAD MAP TO ORGANIZATION

I think of my time management tools (my work schedule and daily to do list) as road maps to my destination. Without their help, I would be lost. It's vital that you don't underestimate their importance.

Compare this to taking a road trip to Alaska without the road map. Without this essential guide to your destination, you're likely to take a whole lot of scenic detours as you zigzag your way across country. Even if you did get lucky and somehow bumbled your way through Canada and into Alaska, you would no doubt have spent more time and money than necessary. A good road map (time management plan) would have led you to your destination by the most direct route and in the quickest, most economical way. So, cherish your time management road maps and quit killing your time.

DOING YOUR DAILIES — GETTING INTO A ROUTINE

Each of us has things we need to take care of on a daily, rather than weekly, basis. These things include meal preparation and cleanup, making beds, making school lunches, and so forth. I do not think it is necessary to clutter your weekly work schedule by listing each of your daily chores. I do, however, think it is useful to establish a routine for getting them done. Let's look at these daily jobs and ideas for making them routine.

Making the bed. The best and most logical time to make your bed is as soon as you get up. (Of course, if someone is still in the bed, this sort of efficiency may work against you.) If you develop the good habit of prompt bed-making, it becomes something done as a matter of routine, and it is one less thing to worry about having to do later. If you have a spouse who sleeps later than you, it becomes his job to make the bed. The logical rule is the last one out is the one to make it. Of course, if you get up together, you can make it together and get the job done quickly.

Cleaning up after meals. Another good daily habit to develop is cleaning up shortly after each meal. If you have difficulty with this, just remind yourself that it has to be done sometime. Waiting only makes it harder. (Once food dries on pots and plates, you practically need explosives to get it off.) If necessary, assess the way you cook and make adjustments. Make a conscious effort to use fewer bowls and utensils. Since the cooking is done by the oven, use that time for cleaning. Fill the sink with soapy water, let the dishes soak, put food back in the fridge, and wipe down the counters. Spend some time on planning and strategy to make things less time-consuming in the long run.

General pick up. Even families with the best intentions can end the day with various things scattered throughout the house. I recommend that you deal with these things in the evening so that you can wake up to a tidy house. If you wind up with quite a few things to put away each night, grab a basket (a laundry basket will work) and

The Enemies of the Organized

Clutter. In my opinion, clutter is the number one (and two and three) enemy of the organized. Unfortunately, this is one lesson that is hard for many people to learn. As a result, their things eventually take over their lives and . . . well, you know the rest. (See chapter two for help in dealing with clutter.)

Lack of Focus. Have you ever had one of these days: First, the dishwasher breaks down, so you can't clean the kitchen. The repair service can't say precisely when someone will get there, so you can't leave to do the grocery shopping. While you wait, you decide to vacuum, but you're interrupted by a call from one of those nice telemarketers. By the time you order five genuine petrified lava chips, the repairman is asking to be paid. After you finally find your handbag (under a pile of clothes — are they clean or dirty?), you realize you've used the last check and you can't find more. You write him an I.O.U. on the first piece of paper you find and march off to the kitchen to finish up. You're out of detergent, because you didn't get to go to the store, and now your kids are home from school demanding a snack. That night at 10:00 P.M., when everybody you know in the free world is preparing for bed, you finally make your trip to the grocery store. You can't remember half the things you wanted. You don't have your list. (That was the piece of paper you gave to the repairman.) When you arrive home exhausted, you trip over the vacuum and sprain something. You'll have to put off doing the dishes. You forgot the detergent.

continued

systematically go through the living areas of your home collecting items in the basket. (This could be an assigned job.) As you move from room to room, return these items to their proper homes. You may either put them where they belong or leave them in the owners' rooms for them to deal with. If you have a willing family, this job should become easier as everyone develops the "Don't put it down, put it away" attitude.

Bathroom tidiness. For most families it's not practical (or desir-

Lack of a Plan. This is probably the main reason you don't stay focused. Like our friend above, there's really nothing to focus on. The day is a lot of unrelated bits and pieces. Take heart, this book is your plan.

Indecision. You don't know what to do, so you do nothing. This is a direct result of not having a plan.

Failure to Make and Take Time. You have time to get your hair done, time to watch "I Love Lucy" reruns, and time to waste searching for misplaced items. You have no time, or so you think, for planning and strategy.

Lack of Routine. Without a routine, you can't be certain things will get done. You only do them when you get a chance.

That Feeling of Being Overwhelmed. Some people take on more than they can handle at a given time in their lives. (This is particularly common among those of us who have a difficult time saying no.) Organized people understand what they can reasonably expect from themselves.

able) to deep clean the bathroom every day. There are, however, a few quick things that can be done in a matter of minutes that give the impression of cleanliness. The person on bathroom duty (more later) should do this routinely in the morning, after everyone is finished in the bathroom. First, rinse out the sink. Wipe it and dry the counter. Next, use a paper towel to wipe the chrome free of watermarks. Last, wipe the mirror. This process takes less than two minutes, but the bathroom will seem much cleaner.

What other jobs do you need to do on a daily basis? Think about how you can establish a routine for getting them done.

ESTABLISHING NEW HABITS—THE 21 DAY RULE

As you begin to use time management tools, get into a routine for daily work, and establish other good habits, remember that the weight of the previous habit (killing time, lack of direction) may pull against you, urging you to resist the new behavior. I remember learning in Mr. Gwynn's high school psychology class that it takes a minimum of twenty-one days to establish a habit. (I must say, I think bad habits take considerably less time.) If you are trying to establish a good habit (such as making and using a daily to do list), you may find times when you must force yourself to do it until at least three weeks pass. You simply are not being fair to yourself if you don't give yourself enough time to let it get under your skin. For instance, once I got into the habit of making my bed every day, it practically drove me crazy not to do it. Now that's the kind of habit I want.

KEEPING TRACK OF IT ALL—YOUR PERSONAL PLANNER

Where do I keep my to do list and all the other tidbits of information I need to keep track of? Well, like many people, I was accustomed to purchasing personal appointment notebooks. I was never satisfied with these, because they are usually cluttered with categories I do not need and do not have enough of those I want.

For this reason, I am very happy with the do-it-yourself styles now available. Rather than buy a notebook with categories that someone else thinks you need, you can now purchase a notebook and select the filler pages from a variety of categories. For instance, if you want to keep vital telephone numbers with you at all times, you can buy the telephone pages. You probably also want some to do lists, already titled so. You may need some blank pages for jotting down notes and ideas, and perhaps a monthly calendar so you have an overview of upcoming events. I also suggest an ongoing list to keep track of the things you need (such as various organizing tools) or want (such as new furniture).

I like this personalized system because you can experiment with a variety of combinations until you get what you want. I caution you to avoid like the plague anything you don't think you will use regularly. If you have no need for keeping phone numbers in your personal planning notebook, don't. Unnecessary categories only bog down the system and make it difficult to use.

These time management tools are a few of the basic organizing tools I referred to earlier. They will help you get where you want to go. Though they may seem foreign to you now, give them a chance. If you let them, they will prove to be helpful in your quest for good organization.

CHAPTER TWO

GETTING CLUTTER OUT OF YOUR WAY

IDENTIFYING AND DEFEATING THE THREE

PRIMARY ENEMIES OF ORGANIZATION —

CLUTTER, CLUTTER

AND CLUTTER

ould you treat your enemies like friends? Would you bring them into your home, care for them, pay their way, and arrange your life to accommodate them? I bet you've been doing it for years. Sound preposterous? Let me show you how it happens everyday.

You've invited some friends to come live with you. Let's say you enjoyed their company for a time. Perhaps they were fun to be around and added enjoyment to your life. Perhaps they also made themselves useful and turned out to be handy helpers to have around. Now, let's imagine that one day everything changed. Not only were these friends no longer any help, they weren't even fun anymore. But, after all, they are your friends, and you did invite them. So, you continue to welcome them, care for them, pay their way and, to an extent, arrange your life to accommodate them. You can't ask them to leave; you've invested too much time and money in them.

HAVE YOU BEEN TREATING YOUR ENEMIES LIKE FRIENDS?

Eventually, all this one-sided giving wears on your nerves. You start feeling angry and hurt. You secretly decide that your friends are lazy bums. You hate what they are doing to you. They take advantage of you, but you can't bring yourself to throw them out. That's clearly what they deserve. Everyone tells you so. They're no good, they don't pull their weight. They're useless.

So, who are these friends cum ne'er-do-wells? Just about everybody has them: the scissors that no longer cut; the game that's missing half its pieces; the glove with no mate; the junk drawer full of dead batteries, broken toys, dried-up pens, springs, screws, keys you can't identify, locks you can't remember the combination to.

These once friendly possessions have outlived their usefulness and have become your enemies. They've turned on you and now wreak havoc in your life and home. They get in your way, they crowd your drawers and closets, they fill the attic and basement, and squeeze the car from the garage. They trip you, they fall on you and they waste your time.

Do you tolerate them? If you haven't learned to recognize your enemies, chances are you have been doing just that.

SO WHY THE BIG DEAL?

Clutter is perhaps the number one enemy of the organized. Organized people understand this and have become experts at identifying their enemies and defending themselves. The unorganized are still treating these bums like friends. They are still making excuses for them. The unorganized are still paying the price, and the stakes are high because clutter costs us big.

Clutter costs us time (which is priceless, because it can never be replaced). Have you ever spent ten minutes trying every pen in your junk drawer to find one that works so that you can take a phone message? Perhaps ten minutes doesn't sound crucial, but multiply that by all the other time you spend sidetracked by clutter, and you are killing a lot of time.

Clutter costs us energy. It makes every job harder. Have you ever had to ransack the house, move piles of laundry or stacks of newspapers just to find your car keys? That's a waste of both energy and time!

Clutter costs us financially. Not only do we pay an initial price when we purchase these items, we also pay for their upkeep and maintenance. If we think they're valuable enough, we may even spend money to insure them. Now, that really hurts!

Clutter costs us peace of mind. We can never fully relax when we know we've got a fire hazard in the basement or stacks of magazines we've been meaning to read. Or how about the uneasy feeling that our stuff is so valuable, somebody else is going to try to take it from us? Does that sound familiar?

While Clutter Costs Us, It Pays Others

- The insurance agent collects a fat little check to insure your clutter . . . ah . . . valuables. (My brother-in-law Mike says that buying insurance is like gambling: You're betting the insurance company that you'll be robbed and they're betting that you won't!)
- The thief makes his living parting you from your clutter. (Maybe he's doing you a favor.)
- Auctioneers and junk dealers do quite well convincing clutterbugs to trade their hard-earned money for even more clutter.

You may be saying, "That's all well and good for *some* people, but I don't have a problem with clutter." Want to bet? Let me give you my definition of clutter:

Clutter is anything you own that does not enhance your life on a regular basis (spouses excluded!).

Still want to bet?

WHERE DOES ALL THIS CLUTTER COME FROM ANYWAY?

It comes into our possession in a variety of ways. Just about everyone has obvious clutter: broken gadgets, old magazines, clothes that no longer fit. That's how people tend to define clutter, as *junk*. But clutter comes in a variety of guises. (In fact, some clutter is so cluttery it falls into several of my categories.) I have listed the more infamous types of clutter found around almost any house. See if you can identify them in your own home.

Born clutter. Some things never even had a chance — they were clutter from the get go. Remember the Pet Rock?

I'm taking it with me clutter. Some clutter was actually once a friend. It worked hard for us and made our lives more enjoyable. When its time came, we should have put it to rest. But, in the interest of getting our money's worth, we greedily hang on, because we don't know when we've had enough of a good thing. (Getting your money's worth does not mean taking it to the grave.)

Imposter clutter. This is actually clutter posing as bargains. I witnessed a man purchase several computer monitors for one dollar at an auction. Great deal? Perhaps it would have been if they hadn't been destroyed by fire. They were completely useless; there was nothing to salvage. He just couldn't resist the bargain price. But what *cost* does he pay in moving them, storing them and tripping over them for the next ten years?

Heirloom clutter. Some clutter is inherited. We hang on to the last piece of chipped china from Grandma's set because "it was Grandma's, bless her soul."

By the way, inheriting isn't all one-sided. Parents also inherit junk from their kids. One of my clients raised seven children to adulthood. They had all moved from their parents' home, but had left much of their stuff behind. This woman was afraid to get rid of their things, thinking that they may be important and needed someday. I pointed out that had they been important, the children (all in their thirties and forties) would have taken them by now.

Bestowed clutter. Some clutter is given to us as gifts by well-meaning friends. "The minute I saw those chubby little cupids, I thought of you!" Gee, thanks.

Rabbit clutter. This clutter comes in the guise of collections and collectibles and multiplies fast.

Masqueraders. This is clutter masquerading as good stuff. It may not be *junk*, in the popular sense of the word, but it's still clutter. Lots of things qualify as masqueraders: unused kitchen appliances, musical instruments, and so forth. Items in this category are in good repair but never used.

Atmosphere clutter. This is clutter pretending to be decorating. Atmosphere clutter ranges from candlesticks, vases and plants to coffee table "art."

Someday clutter. This is useless clutter, but we insist that it will come in handy someday: sixteen empty pickle jars, forty-seven cans of dried-up paint (many with colors you painted six years ago) and half-completed hobby projects.

Bob Hope clutter. This is the sentimental "thanks for the memories" clutter that we are emotionally tied to: twenty-seven bags of leftover rice from your wedding, love letters from your fifth-grade sweetheart (what was his name again?).

Snob clutter. Crystal candy dishes and sterling silver platters get used at Thanksgiving and Christmas, but spend the rest of the year collecting dust and getting in your way.

Why the Clatter Over Clutter?

"So, what's the big deal?" you ask. You admit you've got every kind of clutter I mentioned, and you think you can come up with a few categories of your own. So what if you're a pack rat? So what if the basement is full and the attic is overflowing? It's not hurting anybody. Sure about that?

I wouldn't be so presumptuous as to tell you what to get rid of (Well, I might, if I could meet you in person and get a firsthand look at the junk you've been saving!), but perhaps you don't realize how sneaky clutter can be, how much it can interfere with the true enjoyment of life, and how it can keep you from doing many of the things you want. I didn't.

TRUE CONFESSIONS

When I was a young newlywed, my husband's job took him away from home two weeks of every three. I consoled myself in my loneliness by making our house a comfortable home. My desire was to fill our home with beautiful things, with heirlooms. I made purchases intended to be lifetime keepsakes that someday would be passed to our children. I bought fine books, leatherbound classics and fine crystal (snobs). I purchased solid oak furniture that would last three lifetimes and a canopy bed fit for a king. My husband, too, enjoyed filling our home with things he loved, including a collection of over one hundred chess books (rabbits).

Then, there was the decorating. I wanted to create the appropriate atmosphere. In our townhouse, the living area was on the second floor to take advantage of the mountain view. There was a vaulted ceiling and a loft in the living room. To enhance the dramatic effect, I filled the area with plants. Pothos cascaded from the loft over the antique grandfather clock to the floor, back up, and to the floor again. I wound the vines through the wooden railing of the loft and draped them down the walls. I painstakingly arranged thick wooden shelves on the walls and covered them with candlesticks, books and plants (atmosphere). Even the bathrooms were beautiful.

I created a truly beautiful home, and I can't remember one person visiting without commenting on its beauty. What I did not understand at that time was that, although I was purchasing fine quality items (masqueraders), I was filling my house with clutter and creating an enormous amount of work for myself.

Those shelves I installed, not to mention the things I purchased to sit on those shelves, needed to be dusted regularly. The oak furniture needed to be oiled in that dry Alaska climate. The crystal that hung so beautifully from my sideboard lost a great deal of sparkly loveliness when allowed to gather dust.

In every corner of every room in my home, I had created a beautiful setting. When the house was in order, when everything was cleaned, polished and dusted, it was a delight to behold and enjoy. Of course, I wasn't able to enjoy it. I was confined to bed with a case of exhaustion.

The problem was, although everything was beautiful, it was not particularly functional. I had to do acrobatics to water some of those plants. After a few near-death experiences, I decided I was disinclined to fall (miles) to the floor only to be forced to yell, "I've fallen and I can't get up" to nothing but my precious clutter. My husband would arrive home a week later to discover me thusly. The autopsy would reveal "death by watering (clutter)."

Consequently, the plants missed regular waterings, and their beauty faded as leaves turned yellow and died. I had so many beautiful things on my oak sideboard that dusting them and oiling it became drudgery, and I didn't keep it up as well as I should have. My bathrooms were so beautifully decorated that I had to spend ages just moving things around to scrub them.

It's not that I didn't love my things, but I had learned there was more to life than dusting, polishing, and spending three hours a week watering plants. I wanted to *live* my life, and I finally had to admit to myself that these things of beauty were robbing me of the time I wanted to spend pursuing other interests.

All of this confession of my past sins illustrates a very important point: *Even things of beauty can be clutter.* And this leads to the next important point: *Buy and keep only what you are willing to keep organized and cleaned.* Too much of a good thing = clutter!

SEE FOR YOURSELF

If you are reading this at home right now, stop a moment and look around the room. Take inventory of the various items you can define as clutter. Look with a fresh perspective at things that demand too much of your time and attention. Remember my definition: Clutter is anything you own that does not enhance your life on a regular basis.

Take a moment to list some of these things under the appropriate category. Be honest. This is for your eyes only.

Categorizing Your Own Clutter

Born: _____
The Pet Rock. A chip from the Berlin Wall. That piece of the London Bridge you got in Lake Havasu. Anything that was born to collect dust and take up space. Souvenirs are almost always born clutter.

I'm taking it with me: _____
Anything that has served its purpose and no longer works for you. Used batteries, keys you can't identify, clothes that no longer fit, gadgets with parts missing.

Imposter: _____
Bargains that turned out not to be. Items you bought to fix up for resale, but never did. Even sale items like three cases of shampoo

and forty-two bars of soap. There *will* be other sales, you know!

Heirloom: _____
Grampa's old collection of 78s. Grandma's wedding dress. The steering wheel from Pop's old Model T Ford.

Bestowed: _____
That straw handbag covered with fake fruit, the orange blob they call art, the blouse in a color you can't describe.

Rabbits: _____
Collections of all kinds: books, magazines, state spoons, decorative plates, mushrooms, strawberries, beer cans.

Masqueraders: _____
Zillions of things can fall into this category. Items that are in good repair but never get used. Look around, they're everywhere.

Atmosphere: _____
Plants, candlesticks, sculptures, art, vases, knickknacks, figurines. Anything used to decorate that is overdone or requires too much work to maintain.

Someday: _____
Anything you are not currently using, but you intend to fix, finish or get to someday. Broken appliances, half-painted pictures, clothes that need mending, twenty-seven stacks of newspapers.

Bob Hope: _____
Love letters, high school memorabilia, letterman's sweaters, first flower, wedding invitations. Anything that tugs at your heartstrings and won't let go.

Snob: _____
Crystal saved for company, china used twice a year, sterling silver flatware, platters. Expensive items meant to impress.

How'd you do? Did you need more space? Isn't it amazing how quickly it sneaks up on us? I think everyone should be forced to move once a year until they get out of the clutter habit.

An "Object" Lesson

During the time of my "illness" (my clutter collecting days), I remember shopping at a place that was going out of business and had incredible bargains on beautiful merchandise. I was practically beside myself trying to get hold of as much as I could carry. There were two older women shopping nearby, and I heard one of them tell her friend that she ought to buy the item she was admiring. The friend replied, "It is beautiful, but I don't know where I would put it." I could hardly believe my ears! How could she be so foolish? I thought to myself proudly, "I'd *find* a place."

A couple of years later, I was reminded of that incident when preparing for a garage sale. (Something I hope never to do again.) I had gone into the crawl space under my home and found a cache of things that I had forgotten I had stored there. These things were once much loved and treasured, but not only had I been able to live comfortably without them, I had completely forgotten that I had ever owned them! So much for "finding a place." The woman who had resisted the purchase was much wiser than I.

THINK BEFORE YOU BUY, OR "TO CLUTTER OR NOT TO CLUTTER"

Before you spend your money on something you are not absolutely sure you need or even want, ask yourself these questions:

Is it useful? Does it fill a need that you have at this time? (A spatula is useful, but if you already own five, *put it back!*)

Is it decorative? Do you have a specific place in mind for this item? Are you sure this is the best thing for that spot? Are you willing to do the necessary dusting, polishing, and cleaning associated with owning this item?

Is it compatible with your family? If it's a collection of delicate figurines and you have three small boys, wait a few years. It's more important that your children are comfortable in their home than for you to make a comfortable home for clutter.

Are you only interested because it's such a great deal? Bargains can be anything but, if they are not put to good use working for you, they aren't really bargains. Remember the monitors?

What would happen if you didn't buy it today? Is this a once-in-a-lifetime chance or could you think about it and come back another day? (Even if you forget all the other questions, remember this one. It works.)

Will it make you smarter, wiser, healthier? Buy it.

Can you live without it? Then do.

ARE YOU CRYING "UNCLE" YET?

I know it's difficult for most people to get rid of the clutter in their lives and homes. If you find that you are struggling with the concept of eliminating your precious clutter, do this exercise: Ask yourself, Why am I keeping this? Lame excuses usually fall within one of these familiar categories:

Lame excuse #1. It may come in handy someday. What makes someday any different than today? (Except that someday, like tomorrow, never comes. All you really have is today.) If you haven't needed it during the last year, chances are you won't need it someday.

Lame excuse #2. I could do a little work on it, and it would be as good as new. Like the Victrola you've been meaning to find a needle for? If this is your excuse, what are you waiting for?

Lame excuse #3. It's my lucky _____. Oh, *please!* I suppose you carry seven rabbits' feet and a Lucite-encased four-leaf clover. What are you, a leprechaun?

Lame excuse #4. I spent good money on that! As opposed to what? Bad money?

Lame excuse #5. As soon as I throw it out, I know I'll need it. You won't need it. Chances are you won't even remember it in a few months.

Lame excuse #6. I think it may be worth something. Great! Sell it and get something useful, like organizing tools.

Lame excuse #7. I'm going to read those old newspapers and magazines as soon as I have time. Just how much time do you think you have anyway? Enough to be reading *old* news? Just how long do you expect to live?

I suppose there are nearly as many lame excuses for keeping clutter as there are clutterbugs. If you are using any of the lame excuses above, then there's a 99 percent chance it is clutter. The bottom line is that clutter does you absolutely no good. Do yourself one of the biggest favors in your life, let go and be free!

TO OWN OR BE OWNED

I've noticed that some people just like to own things. They seem to think there's some special meaning in possessing things and being able to say "I own that, that's mine." The trouble is, all the people I have known with this particular personality trait seem to rely on owning things as a way of making up for some other area of their life (like character) that is deficient. They seem to believe that by owning enough material objects they will be considered more important, acceptable or likable. Or perhaps they just enjoy the feeling of envy that is often generated by being an owner. Personally, I don't want anyone to ever feel bad or envious about some thing I own.

Another problem with all of this ownership is that sometimes the line between who is the owner and who is the ownee becomes very fine. Have you ever known anyone who was under tremendous stress trying to keep up with the pursuit of ownership? How many marriages have ended over financial problems stemming from a desire to own?

Don't get me wrong, I'm not saying that all possessions are bad. In fact, many are useful and fun and a delight to have around. But when and if you find yourself working more for your possessions than they are for you, you've lost the battle. You are owned, and that means you have willingly sold yourself into slavery in the one country that above all stands for freedom.

UNCLE!

Now that I've finally got you crying "uncle," and you are ready to dispose of at least some of your clutter, you may feel a bit confused about what to get rid of and what to keep. Ultimately, this is a personal choice, but use my guidelines for help. (Be encouraged to know that you will probably improve at clutter-eliminating skills as time passes.) If you are serious about making this change, I encourage you to go through the house and snap a few photos. It will be great to have "before" pictures to refer back to when you finally get rid of the clutter.

WHAT DO I KEEP?

As you go through your house eliminating clutter, you may find yourself asking, "Should I keep this?" Ask yourself:

- Would I even ask this question if it really was important or useful?
- Have I used this in the last three months? If it's not getting used, it's *useless*. (Seasonal items are excluded.)
- Why don't I use it? Is it broken, missing a part, the wrong size? Perhaps it would be useful to someone else.
- What's the worst thing that would happen if I threw it away? Would I be arrested? Would my family disown me? Relatively few things are irreplaceable. Chances are, if you ever did need it again, it could be replaced.
- How would I get rid of it?
  1. Have a garage sale. Use the money you make to purchase the tools you'll need to establish and maintain organization.
  2. Throw it away. If it's broken, worn out, missing parts.
  3. Give it away. If it doesn't fit you, it may fit someone else. Help the needy. The Salvation Army and Goodwill can use good quality clothing and household items. They may even be able to pick it up for you.

But what about my Bob Hope's and the somedays? You can't expect me to part with them, you cold, heartless woman!

Hey, now! That's enough name calling. I know that eliminating clutter can be a difficult and heartrending process. (I've been there, remember?) I don't expect you to be able to evict all of your clutter at once. I mean, how will you ever get rid of your masqueraders when you get emotional over your somedays? Learning to let go is a process that takes months, even years, to master.

And, even if you did get rid of the clutter, there are still seasonal, sentimental and seldom-used items — the clothes, the snowman Jello mold and the Christmas tree-shaped ice cube trays. And how about the waffle iron you only use on your anniversary? (The tradition is so much fun, you can't give it up.) There will probably always be things that you want to keep, but that won't have a place in the mainstream of your home. So, for all the somedays that you still think you'll get to and all the heirlooms you can't bear to part with, I offer a simple solution. Rather than shoving these things under the bed, stuffing them into closets, or piling them in the garage, store them in one easily accessible storage place. Give your storable items their own home in the box storage system.

What's a box storage system? Read the next chapter to find out.

The clutter will always be among you, at least to an extent, because that's life. You'll probably never rid yourself of every ounce of clutter, and the battle to do so will be an ongoing one. But if you promise yourself to make a habit of routinely throwing away broken things, refusing to become a collector, rejecting useless purchases, and refusing to become emotionally attached to your stuff, you're on your way. Your box storage system will help you when your courage falters.

The Organizer's Pledge

I, (state your name), do solemnly swear, in the presence of God and 113 brown paper bags, 59 empty pickle jars, and 17 pairs of bell-bottom jeans, to rid myself and my home of clutter. I want to live my life, not waste it shuffling clutter. I want to be known for my contributions, not my closets. I refuse to go to my grave buried six feet under *clutter*.

Signed _____ Date _____

Congratulations! You're on your way!

CHAPTER THREE

·THE BOX STORAGE SYSTEM

A SIMPLE SOLUTION TO THE

"I CAN'T LIVE WITHOUT MY JUNK!"

PROBLEM, AND THE FIRST STEP

TO GETTING ORGANIZED

*I*n the previous chapter, I promised you a simple solution to your "I can't live without my junk, no matter how useless it is" problem. Aside from your clutter, there are all sorts of things that are perfectly reasonable to hang on to. The problem is, what do you do with these things? The solution, of course, is a storage system.

Like most people, your storable items probably fall into a few main categories:

1. Things that you rarely need, but want to be able to get to, such as old paperwork and sentimental keepsakes.

2. Items that you want to use, but only occasionally, such as holiday and other seasonal things.
3. Items that you use fairly regularly, but have no place for in the traditional storage areas around your home.

Regardless of their status, you have to give these things a home. Your current solution — to jam them under the bed, cram them into closets and stack them in expensive storage units — just isn't practical. What you need is an orderly system for storing and retrieving this stuff. The answer? A box storage system.

WHAT'S A BOX STORAGE SYSTEM?

A box storage system is simply a set of boxes shelved as a unit in which you store items that you want to keep but:

1. Have no room for in the mainstream of your home.
2. Seldom use.
3. Are seasonal.
4. Are sentimental.
5. Are duplicates.
6. Have no idea what to do with. (The brass lamp in the shape of Texas from Uncle Elmo.)

The box storage system creates a designated home for the odds and ends that would otherwise be overflowing from your closets, drawers and cupboards. Chances are, you have at least some of these things in boxes already. The question is, "Could you find them (immediately) if you needed them?"

Most likely the answer is no. Even if you did have a vague notion where to find something, the boxes would probably be stacked to the ceiling and impossible to get to. Using a box storage system alleviates these problems. There's nothing fancy or mysterious about it; anyone can set one up. The beauty of it is having easy access to the contents, and its orderly function.

So, your box storage system is a convenient way to contain items that you want on a semi-regular basis, as well as those you rarely need. Let's look at some of the things you may want to store there.

Box Storage System Categories

- [ ] art supplies
- [ ] auto care items
- [ ] baby clothes
- [ ] books
- [ ] boots, galoshes
- [ ] camera equipment
- [ ] camping items
- [ ] canning supplies
- [ ] children's papers/art
- [ ] church info
- [ ] craft supplies
- [ ] extra first aid
- [ ] extra kitchen items
- [ ] extra linens
- [ ] extra pantry items
- [ ] greeting cards/stationery
- [ ] high school yearbooks
- [ ] hobby items
- [ ] holiday decorations
- [ ] household tools
- [ ] loose photos/albums
- [ ] magazines
- [ ] maternity clothes
- [ ] old paperwork
- [ ] party supplies
- [ ] picnic basket/supplies
- [ ] pool supplies
- [ ] record albums/tapes
- [ ] reference materials
- [ ] seasonal clothing
- [ ] sentimental baby items
- [ ] sentimental items
- [ ] sewing items
- [ ] sheet music
- [ ] skates
- [ ] ski boots/gloves
- [ ] sports paraphernalia
- [ ] toys
- [ ] trophies/ribbons
- [ ] vacuum accessories
- [ ] volunteer work/club
- [ ] warranties/receipts
- [ ] winter hats/scarves/gloves
- [ ] wrapping paper, bows

What categories could you add?

- [ ] _____
- [ ] _____
- [ ] _____
- [ ] _____
- [ ] _____
- [ ] _____

Let's look at some of these more closely.

Extra kitchen items. The Bundt pan you only use five or six times a year. The three extra spatulas you got on sale. Gizmos and gadgets you seldom use, but can't bring yourself to part with. Free up some of your valuable kitchen space and store these things in the box storage system.

Vacuum cleaner accessories. Do you have attachments you only use a few times a year? Do they fall on your head each time you open the broom closet? Store them here.

Maternity clothes/baby clothes. No sense taking space in your closet or drawers with these.

Camera equipment. Perhaps you have several lenses or a seldom-used flash attachment. Keep them stored in a box.

Old paperwork. Everyone has paperwork they want to keep but seldom need to refer to. Marriage certificate, canceled checks, high school diploma, and old tax returns to name a few.

Sentimental baby items. Baby's first shoes and hospital band, for example.

Hobby/craft. Have you got hobby items you've been meaning to get to? Here's a convenient place to store them until someday.

Wrapping paper and accessories. This is one of my favorite boxes. I always purchase folded paper so that I can store it in the boxes. I've got paper, ribbons, bows, tape and scissors. I can grab the box, and I've got everything I need. Toss it back in, and back onto the shelf it goes.

Picnic basket. If you enjoy picnics, keep a box with the basic supplies ready to go. Plastic or paper plates, garage sale silverware, napkins and tablecloth.

Greeting cards/stationery. Keep a few birthday cards and others on hand for last-minute remembrances.

IMMEDIATE BENEFITS

The wonderful thing about using a box storage system is that you can keep most of your storables together. No more wondering, "Where could it be?" (The attic, basement, hall closet, under the bed, in the garage and so forth.)

While the box storage system is an indispensable tool, it is not to be abused. Don't use it as an excuse to save and store every piece of junk you've ever owned. You want to be selective with the items you store there. Always eliminate everything you possibly can, and resort to the box storage system only when you absolutely must keep something.

Another benefit of the box storage system is that it helps you softies who have a hard time letting go of things. If you store something in the box storage system, you have the security and peace of mind of knowing that you still possess your precious clutter and, better yet, can put your finger on it when and if you need it. (Can you honestly say that now?) You may be surprised, however, to find that you can live perfectly well without these things, and after a year of residing unused in the box storage system, it may be easier for you to let go altogether. (We can only hope and pray.)

EASY TO SET UP

There is no standard format to the box storage system; adapt the concept to your circumstances and needs. It's a good idea to guesstimate how many boxes you require (double that figure for a more accurate count), then determine a suitable place to set it up. Some suggestions are the garage (unless you have a pest problem), a spare bedroom or guest room, laundry room, sewing room, utility room, attic or basement. You want it to be handy without getting in the way. For the type of shelves to use, there are a few different options:

1. Use a set or two of metal utility shelves.
2. Make or contract for a set of wood shelves.
3. Use an existing closet, adding shelves if necessary.
4. Use plywood shelves on blocks.

It doesn't matter how you house the boxes, as long as the shelves are sturdy. Look around your house and find a suitable place, and this will help dictate the method you use.

Tips

• Purchase new cardboard boxes. This way, they will be fresh and give a clean, orderly appearance.

I think appearance is important for the psychological effect. If you have old, dirty or scribbled on boxes, it takes away from the feeling of order. Boxes are not very expensive, and you can find them by checking your Yellow Pages. (Look under "Boxes.")

If possible, purchase them directly from a box manufacturer. If there isn't one in your town, the closest big city may have one that can ship boxes directly to you. I suggest you purchase them from the manufacturer rather than a secondary source such as do-it-yourself movers, because the latter will likely charge more. The price will probably depend on the number you buy, and you may have to buy a minimum number (probably twenty-five). This will not be too many. In addition to using them for storage, you will need extra boxes for the organizing and sorting process. (More in chapter four.) For a neat appearance, I recommend that all the boxes be the same size.

• It doesn't matter how many boxes you have, but if you wind up with one hundred, I think you need to do some serious eliminating. An average family could easily have twenty-five to thirty boxes.

• When you receive the boxes, they will be flat. You will need a way to enclose the bottom. For storing lightweight items, use the standard overlapping fold method. For boxes that will contain heavier items, use heavy duty tape or a hot glue gun and glue sticks. If you decide to use hot glue, please be very careful. Taping is easier, but may look messy if not carefully applied. Ask the manufacturer for recommendations.

• When you are ready to label the boxes, be neat. Use sticky pad sheets, or $3'' \times 5''$ cards and apply them to the end of the box with two-sided tape. I prefer this method to marking the box, because it's neater and the contents may change periodically.

• Use general categories such as those listed above. Do not attempt to list every item in the box. Just use the broad category name.

• Do not store more than one category in each box. This only invites confusion.

• I recommend that the boxes be at least sixteen inches long, but no longer than twenty-four inches. They should be ten to twelve inches high and about the same in width.

• I have used different methods for housing my boxes, depending on the particular situation in my home at the time. I currently use metal shelves that are eighteen inches deep and boxes that are eighteen inches long by twelve inches high by twelve inches wide. This size works well, but choose what you like. It's best if they don't hang over the shelf, so take that into consideration when you purchase shelves. I have seen metal shelves as deep as twenty-four inches.

I have found the box storage system to be an invaluable aid in establishing and maintaining organization at my house. I wouldn't attempt to organize without it. I think you will enthusiastically agree, once you give it a try.

CHAPTER FOUR

PREPARING TO TACKLE THE JOB

THE TOOLS AND METHODS

OF GETTING ORGANIZED,

INCLUDING A THREE-STEP

ORGANIZATIONAL METHOD

THAT LEADS TO

STREAMLINED LIVING

*E*very profession has its tools. Where would your doctor be without her little black bag? How far would your dentist get without his drill? Just as these tools are essential to their trades, certain tools are essential for your profession of home management and organization. Not using the proper tools or trying to cut corners just doesn't cut the mustard.

TOOLS AND TIPS

Have you ever tried to cut the grass with kitchen shears? Of course not. The very idea is preposterous. Well, technically, you probably could do it, but it would no doubt take pretty close to forever. And then there's the likelihood of throwing out your back, not to mention your knees, and your neighbors might look at you funny. But, it could be done.

Still, the question remains: Why would you? The obvious answer is that you wouldn't. That's what lawnmowers are for. While an argument could be made for the cost-effectiveness of shears over lawnmowers, the opposing side could cite the cost of medical bills certain to arise from cutting the grass the "cheap" way.

While all of this is absolute nonsense, I have seen much the equivalent in people struggling to get organized. They are frustrated by disarray, but they are not getting anywhere, because they do not understand the importance of having and using the proper organizing tools.

WHAT ARE THESE TOOLS?

Below is a list of tools I would like you to gather. None of them is particularly expensive, but they are all invaluable organizing aids.

Your Box Storage System (AKA Clutter Corral)

In chapter three you learned about the box storage system. It is a simple way of organizing most of your storables in one area. I can't emphasize enough the importance and usefulness of this tool. Please do not attempt to proceed without having your box storage system set up and ready to go. You will be using it immediately.

Your Sorting Boxes

These will help tremendously. As you sort through rooms, closets and drawers, you will be able to deal immediately with each item you come across. This simple technique makes the whole job run smoothly. Don't make the mistake of thinking you don't need to bother with this step. It only takes a moment to gather your boxes and saves a lot of needless running around later.

Get four boxes, such as those used for your box storage system (large baskets or paper bags in a pinch), and mark each with one of these four categories:

Put away. This box is for items you will come across that need to be put away in their proper home. (Roller skates you find in the kitchen cupboard, bills under the couch cushions, etc.) If you stopped to put away each item as you came across it, you would never get your job completed. Toss any out-of-place items into this box, and work on them after your initial job is complete.

Give away. *Be generous!* This box, obviously, is for items that you are willing to part with. If you are planning to give items to a charity, please be thoughtful. Don't give broken items or stained or ripped clothing.

By the way, if you traditionally have had difficulty letting go of things, it is important that you move the give-away items out of your house as soon as possible. If you leave them hanging around, you will only be tempted to dig through them again. This could spell disaster.

Throw away. Be generous here, too. This may be your largest collection.

Store away. This box is for items you plan to keep, but need to get out of the mainstream of your home. Store these items in your box storage system.

Note: If you think you are energetic enough to hold a garage sale, you may want to get a fifth box and mark it for sale items. However, before you hold a garage sale, consider whether the money you expect to make will be worth the effort. I've known people who actually spent as much money advertising the sale as they made selling their belongings. If you only plan to charge a dime or a quarter for most of your things, it's probably not worth the time and effort involved. Give the items to charity instead.

If you do decide a garage sale is worth the effort, use the money for organizing supplies. Promise yourself that you'll give away any leftovers promptly.

Your Need and Want List

If you have set up a personal planning system (chapter one), your need and want list will be part of that. If you haven't done that yet, plan to have paper and pencil handy for jotting things down as you think of them.

Other Tools of the Trade

Most of your tools are relatively small, relatively inexpensive things such as baskets and trays for corralling various items and organizing devices such as tie holders and shoe bags. These will help you organize and contain your belongings. As we progress, I will mention other tools and their uses.

I would like you to view your organization tools with the same high regard you give to your other tools. They are every bit as valuable, maybe more so. Just as your lawn and garden equipment is an investment that helps to maintain the value of your property, your organizing tools are a valid and valuable investment in comfort, peace of mind and sanity. Since I'm not talking about huge sums of money, the return on your investment will far outweigh the cost.

The Work Area—Command Central

If possible, designate a room (such as a seldom-used guest room or even a corner of the basement), as command central. This is the place to store your four boxes when you are not using them. This is also the area to keep your garage sale and give-away items. Don't be discouraged if this area sometimes resembles an explosion at a flea market. The bigger your pile, the better. It's an indication that you are serious about getting organized and are willing to cut the clutter out of your life. Remember it's better to get rid of the give-away items immediately to avoid temptation.

HOW IT ALL WORKS

As you proceed through your home, you will be organizing rooms and spaces by following three basic organizing steps: designate, eliminate and contain. Let's look at each of these a little closer.

Step One: Designate

Designate the purposes of each room or space. You can't begin to organize a space until you know what you want to do with it. I will provide a list of common purposes for each area we cover. As you review the list, simply check off the items that apply to your situation. I have also provided space for you to jot down additional ideas.

Step Two: Eliminate

During this phase, you will use your sorting boxes. Once you determine the purposes for an area, you automatically can see what no longer meets those designated purposes and, therefore, what needs to be eliminated from the space. Eliminating unnecessary items is one of the most helpful things you can do to establish and maintain organization. Even among the items you want to keep, it is advisable to eliminate the duplicates. (Those five extra spatulas!) These can be kept in your box storage system.

Step Three: Contain

Once you have designated the purposes for an area and eliminated as much as possible, you need to create a specific home for the items that remain. This part is fun! Have your need/want list handy during this phase to jot down ideas for organizers and other tools you can add to make the area more efficient. Once everything has been given a home, label the shelves, cupboard doors or containers to help maintain order. It really does work.

WHEN THE BOXES ARE FULL

Once you have organized an area and your boxes are full, you may wonder how to dispose of the contents.

The throw-away box. The throw-away box is easy enough to dispatch. Of course, if you have large amounts of throw-away items, plan to make regular trips to the local recycling bins or dump.

The put-away box. If you find you only have a few items to return to their proper homes, then please do so immediately. If you are reluctant to start because the pile is so high or because you haven't got anything that even vaguely resembles a proper home, then store these items at command central until you are organized enough to ease them back into your house. With this method, you will need plenty of boxes on hand.

The give-away box. These items can be transferred to a large plastic garbage bag and stored at command central. As I said before, it's wise to get them out of the house as soon as possible.

The store-away box. These items will go into your box storage system, so be very choosy about what goes in here. When you are ready to sort items into your box storage system, do so by establishing broad categories (see chapter three). Rather than mark a box with each individual item, mark it with the general topic. *Kitchen* encompasses anything that is considered a kitchen item. If you need something, you will know to check that box. There is no need to list the contents (two egg cups, Christmas Jello mold, glass casserole, and so forth). That's too time-consuming, and the contents will change from time to time.

The garage sale box. You may find it easier to leave things in boxes until you get ready to sort and price them for the sale. If you do, you will need lots of boxes. Store them at command central.

Tips

Plan your organizing sessions. Just as other professionals plan how they will spend their time, you should too. (See chapter one.)

Dress comfortably. Temperature permitting, it's easier to work in short sleeves. Choose an outfit that is nonrestricting, but presentable, just in case someone stops by. A lightweight sweat suit could work — push up the sleeves. You don't have to look like a movie star, but you'll probably feel better if your hair is combed. Also, remember to wear comfortable shoes. I have found that there is more spring in my step when I wear a pair of comfortable athletic shoes than when I go barefoot.

Be very specific about what you will be organizing. Instead of saying, "Today I will organize the kitchen," choose a specific aspect to work on. "Today I will organize the refrigerator."

Set a start and stop time. Having a definite stop time planned is helpful, because you know that there is an end in sight. If you take the attitude that you will work until you get the job finished, you may be exhausted and in the midst of a mess by the end of the day. This may only discourage you from getting started the next time. If you set a stop time, you can be satisfied that you have successfully completed your day's work.

Work on the outside appearance first. If you want to work on organizing the bedroom closet, first be sure that the bed is made and laundry is off the floor. The improved appearance and sense of order will give you an immediate lift.

Begin with the smallest item in the room. For instance, tackle the nightstand as opposed to the closet. When doing general pickup, it's probably easier to work the room in a right-hand direction if you are right-handed and left-hand direction if you are left-handed. An efficiency expert suggested this, and it does seem to prevent back-tracking.

Always clean up. Even if you plan to work on a project the next day, always clean up. Plans change, things come up, and tomorrow turns into next week. If you leave a mess in sight, you'll feel guilty each time you walk by. Worse yet, you might get used to it. Plan your cleanup so that it is finished by your stop time.

Pay attention to your energy level. Become aware of your high and low energy times. If it would be helpful, take notes for a week or two so you can see a pattern. Don't waste the possibility of a productive accomplishment by gabbing on the phone.

Be realistic. Don't expect to get a whole room organized in one day. Every room has several components. Concentrate on one aspect or one component of that room. Be satisfied with your progress. Remember, you are making a lifestyle change here, and it's going to take some time.

Finally, I want to leave you with this thought. Here's a little verse I made up, and I think it is rather applicable to goal setting. Remember it especially when your energy is waning:

> Persistence brings results,
> results bring satisfaction,
> satisfaction brings renewed energy.

Ready? Set? Get Organized!

CHAPTER FIVE

HELP FROM YOUR FAMILY

ELEVEN PRACTICAL WAYS

TO GET SUPPORT AND *REAL HELP*

FROM THE KIDS AND

FROM THAT SKEPTICAL SPOUSE

Well, you want to get organized. You want help, or at least cooperation, from your family. That's natural. (Foolhardy, but natural.) You realize, of course, that they may not be forthcoming with gracious assistance.

Most likely, your family views this as just another one of your crazy "kicks." They've probably already held an emergency meeting to map out their strategy. They speculate that if they just keep their noses clean and lay low for a while, the whole thing will blow over in a couple of weeks.

Boy, do you have news for them! Unlike the tofu diet, the A.M. aerobics, and the vegetable garden for a healthy heart, *this* time you mean business! This is important, really important, to you and you intend to make this improvement. After all, you are doing it for their benefit as well as your own. You want them to change for their own good, to lead more fulfilling lives . . .

GET REAL!

Yeah, yeah, all that's well and good, but let's talk about the real world for a minute. I'm no fan of afternoon talk shows, but I've seen enough of those psychologists to know that we really can't change another person, let alone an entire family. Just because you're gung ho about getting organized doesn't mean that anybody else will be.

With that understanding, I offer you some guidelines. I think that among a reasonable group of people, these steps should prove rewarding. (But then, we're dealing with your family now, aren't we? Have the words *reasonable group of people* ever been used in association with that bunch?) I digress.

Follow my suggestions and maybe you will see some cooperation (eventually), but don't be terribly disappointed if you don't. Go into this with your eyes wide open, so you won't be discouraged midway. You really have to do this for yourself, although naturally you believe you are doing it for the good of your entire family. Quite so. If your family turns out to be unappreciative and maddeningly apathetic, you still need to carry on for your own peace of mind. Got it? Good!

HELP FROM CHILDREN

You may or may not be in a very good position to elicit help from your kids. If your house is a wreck and has been for years, and your children are teenagers who grew up accustomed to this mode of living, run for your life. All right, I realize that's a pretty dim prediction, but the truth is, it just may be too late.

Actually, I'm an eternal optimist, with the staunch belief that if one is still breathing, there's hope. However, the older we get, the more set in our ways we become. While teens don't actually have one foot in the grave, they certainly are old enough to have very definite opinions. As a parent, it's your right and responsibility to require a certain amount of cooperation from them. If you have never done so in the past, however, don't expect change overnight. In fact, you may have to face the awful truth that the example you've been setting all these years has worked. They can make (and ignore) messes with the best of them.

If you follow the steps below and still get no response, console yourself with the thought that your teenagers will soon be leaving the nest. After they have gone, you can have things the way you want. (Of course, you'll miss them and their messes like crazy.)

Help From Little Ones

Little children, on the other hand, may be full of promise. Toddlers love to imitate adults, and while you won't expect any actual help from them, you can lay the groundwork for many years of cooperation to come. When your little one is under foot, seemingly in your way, take the opportunity to plant some productive seeds. He is just anxious to "help" mummy, so let him think that he is doing just that.

When you dust, give him a little rag or washcloth and let him "dust," too. Child proof your house so he won't be in danger of breaking a figurine or vase and hurting himself. If you have delicate things, assign him a specific and safe area to dust. When you sort laundry, let him help sort whites from darks. When you put clothes away in dresser drawers, let him help, even if a few things get unfolded. When you vacuum, let him run his toy lawnmower alongside.

Whatever you are doing, try to include your child in some safe, simple way. Make sure you offer lavish praise and plenty of frequent hugs and kisses so that he knows his help is appreciated. Whatever you do, don't fuss and groan about him being in the way or send him off to play while you get your work done. Doing so will only give him an unpleasant feeling about work and contributing. That mistake will cost you dearly in the long run.

Children in grade school may be your best helpers. They are still young enough to like you and want to spend time with you. Also they probably won't be as busy as their older siblings who are involved with jobs, sports, clubs, and other activities. If you encourage their interest as toddlers, and elicit their help at the grade-school level, you will not only be doing yourself a favor, you will be helping them. Giving them a solid foundation for organization, clean comfortable living and cooperative teamwork is a wonderful gift from parent to child. All those attributes will help them in their adult lives.

As to what to actually expect from your children at any age only you can answer. You know your children better than anyone. You know what they are capable of and what would be too much. When possible, team up a younger one with an older one so they can learn, but won't have an undue burden. If you think a task is too tough for them, then you do it. Children can do easier jobs now, and in a few years, may be able to take on more responsibility.

Just remember, children are not our servants. Include them because they are part of the team and learning these things helps prepare them for adulthood. Chipping in with work may also dispel the fantasy that adult life is all fun. (Remember that one?)

HELP FROM A SPOUSE OR ROOMMATE

This will be tougher. While you have authority over your children, you don't over another adult. Try to remind yourself about his good qualities while you are picking up his socks for the nine thousandth time. Seriously though, you have to approach this with the realization that your spouse may never change.

The question is: Will you love him anyway? (Don't let your hopes get too high and you won't be disappointed.) If he has any sense of fair play, your enthusiasm and good example will persuade him to pitch in. Try to make helping as easy as possible, so there can be no excuses for not cooperating. (But don't expect anyone else to dust the 429 frogs you've been collecting since junior high.)

The chore charts, described later in this chapter, present in black and white the labor necessary to keep a home clean and functioning smoothly. If that doesn't arouse your spouse's sense of fair play, I don't know what will.

Here are your general guidelines. It's up to you to have the fortitude to carry them through.

Affirm your goal and the worthiness of it. You must be certain that this undertaking is something you want and need to do. You can't very well expect help from people who doubt your own commitment. Once you are convinced that getting organized is the right thing to do, no amount of jeering from the sidelines will deter you.

Talk to your family about your goals. This is optional, and your decision will depend on your previous experiences. If your family is in the habit of discouraging you before you even begin a new project, don't tell them right away. Work quietly without drawing a lot of attention to yourself. (Hunh?) Eventually, you may feel comfortable enough to let them in on it.

On the other hand, if you expect encouragement (if not actual help), you may want to let your family know what you're up to. Even if they are not ready to pitch in, they may try to be more considerate about their messes.

Just be sure you concentrate on the use of the word *I* when giving your pitch. *I* need to make a change. *I* haven't been setting the example that *I* should. At this point, you don't want to scare anyone off with a lot of *yous* and *wes*.

Set an example! You can't logically expect your children to clean their rooms when your areas of the house are a constant wreck. If you want to earn their consistent cooperation, you had better be consistent yourself.

Don't be a martyr. If you need plenty of encouragement and back patting, this may be the hardest part for you. Naturally, by making this big change, you want everyone to fuss over you, tell you how wonderful you are, and admire how hard you've been working. You may be tempted (unconsciously, I'm sure) to throw in an extra sigh when family members are about. Well, go ahead, if you must, but you're just going to make everybody sick. Nobody likes a martyr, especially an ostentatious one.

Don't nag. No matter how hard this will be (and it will sometimes feel like torture), don't nag! Naggers are right up there on the popularity scale with martyrs. If you feel you just have to nag someone or you'll go crazy, go into your closet and quietly nag yourself. This will help you understand why nagging doesn't work.

Provide the proper tools. This is essential. You can't very well expect your children to keep their rooms organized if you don't provide them with the proper organizing tools. Give them appropriate storage for toys and plenty of it. Make sure they have laundry baskets for dirty clothes, and so forth.

Be specific about what you want. As your family comes around, be very clear about what you want them to do. Don't give vague instructions such as: "Clean up in here." That only invites philosophical debates as to the true definition of clean. It's better if everyone has a clear understanding of what *your* definition is.

Also, don't expect your family to just see what needs to be done.

HELPER ASSIGNMENTS						
Week of 7-1	7-8	7-15	7-22	7-29	8-5	8-12
Eric laundry	LR FR + entry	kitchen	Bath room	laundry	LR FR + entry	kitchen
Jordan Bath room	laundry	LR FR + entry	kitchen	Bath room	laundry	LR FR + entry
Keegan kitchen	Bath room	laundry	LR FR + entry	kitchen	Bath room	laundry
Amy LR FR + entry	kitchen	Bath room	laundry	LR FR + entry	kitchen	Bath room

Here's an idea for a chart that you could make up to list and rotate the jobs.

What may seem obvious to you won't be to them. Set up an orderly system for keeping track of job responsibilities, so that each person knows what is expected. Make up chore charts (see below) for every area and keep a master list for yourself. (The sample chore charts at the end of some of the chapters may help.)

Teach them. Invest some time in teaching each person how to do each job. You can't ask an adult or a child to clean the bathroom if he has never done so before. Do it together, setting your personal standards and giving explicit directions, safety precautions and guidance on how to safely use and store the cleansers.

Chore charts. These list all the basic cleaning tasks that you want done on a weekly basis. Your chart could also have a shopping list. The person cleaning a bathroom, for example, could note which cleaning supplies are finished or running low. These notes can be checked by your kitchen helper as you prepare your weekly shopping list. Post a chore chart in an inconspicuous location in each room.

Rotate the jobs. If you have several children from whom you expect help, be sure to rotate the jobs you give them on a weekly basis. This should give each child enough time to get the hang of the job without getting too bored. (Don't expect little ones to learn this quickly. Also, they may have forgotten a few things by the time a job rotates back to them on the schedule. Be patient.) It is also very important that job assignments don't fall prey to sexism. Both boys and girls should learn how to take care of themselves, prepare a meal, clean a bathroom, etc.

Offer lots of praise. When a child performs a task properly, or even when a little improvement is in order, be sure to offer lots of encouragement. Make sure you offer correction, not criticism. When a typically unhelpful spouse pitches in, be sure to let him know you appreciate it. Even when you are tempted to say, "Well, it's about time. . . ," don't. You'll only be hurting yourself, because he may never help again.

As you attempt to elicit help from your family members, remember your original goals and why you are doing this. You want an orderly (not sterile) house. You want a comfortable home, not military barracks. You want peace, not constant bickering about who left what where.

Remember that the longer your family has been living with disarray, the longer it may take to get their cooperation and help. Of course, there is the possibility that they may be as tired of it as you are. (You can only hope and pray.) No matter how long it takes, though, you have a worthy goal. Creating a positive environment and setting good examples for our families are always worth the effort.

Good luck!

PART TWO

THE ROOMS

THE TOUR BEGINS

CHAPTER SIX

FOYERS AND ENTRIES — THE FIRST IMPRESSION

MAKING GREAT

FIRST IMPRESSIONS

ON YOUR GUESTS

*H*ave you ever felt like chucking your welcome mat and replacing it with a Do Not Disturb sign? Well, that's not very nice, but it may be just how you feel if you cringe with embarrassment each time someone knocks at your door.

The main entry is like the family tattletale: It keeps no secrets. It's the first impression visitors have of your home and it sets the tone for you and your family as you arrive home.

What kind of a first impression does your entry make? Is it welcoming, pretty and orderly? Or, is it so cluttered and chaotic that it makes you want to leave? (Is it an example of what lies beyond?)

The entry area of a home is thought to say a lot about the people who reside there. If the entry is cluttered, the assumption will be that the rest of the home is cluttered also. If the entry is orderly and welcoming, the impression (right or wrong) is that the rest of the house is orderly, too. Though it may be virtually impossible to keep an entire home spotless at all times, it's not difficult to keep an entry area tidy, particularly if it has been well organized. I suggest you start your home organizing project right here, at the front door. At least if you get your entry organized, you won't have to be mortified every time the doorbell rings!

> **What Your Helper Does**
> - Keeps main entry area swept and dusted.
> - Polishes.
> - Cleans mirror.
> - Distributes incoming mail (Optional).
> - Does same for children's entry.

THE TOOLS OF THE TRADE

Since there is such a variety of entry styles, I thought the best way to teach the organization of this area would be to concentrate on the tools you need to make it function at its optimum. Adapt these tools to your situation. Don't fret if you don't have ideal circumstances; few do. Just do the best you can with what you have.

Remember, too, that you may not be able to use every one of my suggestions. That's OK. At least by using what you can, you will be better off than you are currently.

WHERE DO I START?

When organizing any space, we use our three progressive steps: designate, eliminate and contain. (See chapter four.) These steps are a recurring theme throughout this book and should become second nature to you. To make things easy, I have created a list of the most common needs (purposes) for an entry area. Check off the ideas you want to use.

Step One: Designate the Purposes of the Entry Area and Closet

I want my main entry to have a place for . . .

☐ keys   ☐ shoes and boots
☐ hats, gloves, scarves   ☐ umbrellas
☐ sitting   ☐ slippers
☐ briefcases   ☐ change, gum and other
☐ mail pick-up/send-off   pocket items
☐ broom   ☐ _____
☐ coats and jackets   ☐ _____
☐ mirror   ☐ _____
☐ wastebasket   ☐ _____

On the lines provided, you may add any other designated purposes that you feel you need. Try to keep them closely related to my suggestions. Avoid anything that isn't absolutely necessary (such as sports equipment).

Let's take a closer look at each item on the list. Later, we will see how to make use of these tools in different situations.

A place for keys. Many people waste valuable time searching for keys because they have no permanent home for them. The logical place for keys is near your entry/exit points. I suggest you establish a specific storage place; don't just set them on a hall table. Use a key rack, a hanging basket, or a dish in the hall table drawer.

Jackets and coats. The closet, of course, is the place to store these. If you have young children, customize your closet with a low rod for their convenience. If your entry doesn't have a closet, you will need a coatrack. I prefer wall-mounted over freestanding, because freestanding racks tend to topple easily, take up too much floor space, and are difficult to clean around. If you prefer, you can simply use hooks. In either case, purchase coatracks or hooks with a ball at the end of the hooks to prevent damage to clothes and possible eye accidents.

Hats, gloves and scarves. If you live in a climate that requires these, create a convenient place to keep them. Customizing a closet with cubbyholes for small items is ideal. A cheaper, but no less effective way of containing these items is in a basket. Each member of the family can have his own basket for his personal items, or assign a basket for each category of item. If you want to use baskets, be sure to purchase a stackable style. Since hats and gloves will occasionally be wet, purchase a few coat hangers with clips so you can hang them (outside the closet) while they dry.

Shoes and boots. This is a major concern in harsh climates. Muddy shoes and wet and snowy boots must be removed at the entry so that they don't make tracks all over the house. A rubber mat with a curled edge or a dishpan will contain wet boots and catch the dripping snow.

Slippers. When peeling off wet boots, it's nice to have warm, cozy slippers on hand. Bootie-type slippers don't take up much room and can also be stored in a basket.

Sitting bench. This is an often-overlooked but handy feature in an entry. Sitting is preferable to the typical one-leg balancing act we do when putting on or taking off boots and shoes. Some benches have seats that lift to reveal storage, providing a great place for hats, gloves, and slippers. If a bench is not practical in your circumstances, perhaps a chair would work.

Mail. When you bring mail into the house, it either needs to be distributed to family members or left in a specific place for pick-up. (There is more on mail in chapter fifteen, The Office.) A good tool for mail pick-up and send-off is a basket. To avoid confusion, use one for each category, particularly if you have a lot of mail. Distinguish them by style or by having one on a table and one mounted on the wall.

Umbrellas. You may want to keep an umbrella handy throughout the year. Of course, umbrella stands are available (or use an inexpensive wastebasket), but if you don't have room for one, hang your umbrellas from hooks on the wall or on your coatrack. If possible, leave wet umbrellas open on a covered porch to dry.

Briefcases. If there's room, it's useful to create a place for these. Briefcases should be stored out of sight in a closet or cabinet, so the owners won't have a constant reminder of work or school. This also removes visual clutter and obstacles underfoot.

Pocket items. Ideally, everyone proceeds straight to their rooms to deposit these items. Habits are hard to break, however, and if your family members are accustomed to emptying their pockets when they walk in the door, you need a place to contain these small items so they don't spread like wildfire. Storing them out of sight in a drawer is best. Each person can have her own little container (such as a margarine tub) for gum, change, papers, and so forth. If there is no drawer nearby, contain them in a wall-mounted basket.

Broom. When autumn leaves and winter snowflakes blow their way into our homes, brooms are especially helpful. They don't take up much room, and it is convenient to keep one right at your entry.

Mirror. Having a mirror close by to peek into before you answer the door is a useful feature in an entry. (Have you ever caught a glimpse of yourself after the caller has left?) If there's no practical place to put a large mirror, mount a small one on the inside of the closet door.

Wastebasket. If you have room in the closet or in a corner, keeping a wastebasket in this area is very handy.

Step Two: Eliminate

Once you have a list of designated purposes for your entry area, go through and eliminate the things that no longer meet those purposes. Collect your four boxes and proceed by sorting through the closet and surrounding area. Dispose of your boxes appropriately at command central. (See chapter four.) If you expect this to be a big job, you may want to set a start and stop time.

Step Three: Contain

After everything unnecessary has been eliminated, move to the third step by gathering your needed supplies and organizing what is left.

Because there is such a variety of entryways, let me show you the possibilities with these illustrations.

An entry with no closet. An entry with no closet can look cluttered very quickly. Use the tools and ideas you need. (Refer to the illustration on page 60.)

An entry with a closet. The size of the closet, as well as your family's requirements, will determine what you can accomplish. The key is careful planning. After you've established your needs, sketch a picture of your ideal closet and have a carpenter customize it for you. If this is not feasible, do it yourself by adjusting rod heights and adding hooks, shelves and baskets.

CHILDREN'S ENTRY

This idea may be useful if you have a big family, and you tend to trip over each other as you come and go. This is not intended to make children feel like second-class citizens. You should make it special for them, and customize it to fit their needs.

A door leading to the backyard or play area is a likely candidate for a children's entry. You may prefer to keep coats and other outdoor apparel at the main entry, but use this secondary entrance as the play entry. This is where they come when their boots are muddy, when they come in to grab a toy, and so forth.

Step One: Designate the Purposes of the Children's Entry

The children's entry is a place for . . .

- ☐ lunch boxes
- ☐ school papers, books
- ☐ first-aid kit
- ☐ slippers
- ☐ pocket items
- ☐ broom

☐ artwork	☐ umbrella
☐ coats and jackets	☐ _____
☐ boots and shoes	☐ _____
☐ hats, gloves, scarves	☐ _____

Step Two: Eliminate

Just as with the main entry, you need to gather your four sorting boxes and go through this area, eliminating everything that no longer meets your designated purposes. Once that is complete, move on to arranging and containing.

Lunch boxes. Children should get into the habit of cleaning them when they get home and storing them in a designated place. It makes sense to keep them in the kitchen. If there is absolutely no room there, other options are in the owner's bedroom, in the dining-room hutch, or in a closet in the children's entry.

School papers. If you and your spouse like to review your children's schoolwork, designate a place, such as a special basket, where they can leave their papers for your perusal.

First-aid kit. It may prove handy to keep a first-aid kit near the children's entrance for minor scrapes and scratches. Use discretion with little ones in the house. Avoid putting any potentially dangerous items within their reach.

Artwork. Artwork and other schoolwork your children are proud of should be granted a place of honor. I suggest you display treasured pictures, crafts and tests on a bulletin board designated for this purpose, and they'll feel special and appreciated. Hang it where it will be seen but not get in the way, such as on a kitchen, hall or family room wall.

Teach children to let go of unnecessary paperwork, and help them set up a file for papers to keep. (See chapter nine, Children's Rooms.) Be sensitive to their feelings. They may find it just as difficult to let go as you do.

Tips

- Store outdoor toys such as bats and balls in a plastic garbage can with a lid, right outside the children's entrance.
- Even if you don't have children, keep a few toys on hand for your friends' children to play with while visiting.

- Give a few toys to friends who have no children, so yours will have something to play with when you visit.
- Cleaning should be a rotated job like others.

GARAGE ENTRY

A garage entry can be improved by using many of the tools listed for the main entry. Organize this area by following the same three steps: designate, eliminate and contain.

An additional piece of advice is to get mats that help prevent your family from tracking dirt and dust through the house. Cleaning expert Don Aslett suggests using exterior and interior mats that will each accommodate four strides. This will catch most of the dirt that is normally tracked into the house, so be sure to select mats long enough to accommodate at least four strides by the tallest person in your house. Check your Yellow Pages under Janitorial Supplies to find industrial-style mats for this purpose.

As you assess the tools you will need for your entry areas, you may find that you already have some around the house. Here is a list of items mentioned in this chapter. Use it to help determine what you need for your entry areas. Most of these items are available at discount, variety and houseware specialty stores.

- stackable shelves for shoes and boots
- baskets for scarves, gloves, hats
- a second closet rod or hooks for children's coats
- bench or chair
- basket for booties, socks
- hangers with clips for wet mittens, hats
- rubber mat or plastic tub for boots
- stackable shelves for lunch boxes
- baskets for mail
- key rack or hooks
- first-aid kit
- umbrella stand
- broom and dustpan
- industrial mat for entries

When you get your entryways organized, you may be tempted to put out the old welcome mat again!

CHAPTER SEVEN

THE LIVING AND
FAMILY ROOMS

BRINGING COMFORT AND

ORGANIZATION TO ROOMS

WHERE FAMILIES GATHER

*T*he living and family rooms in a home can be wonderful, comfortable places for the entire family to gather and share a lively discussion, play games, read aloud, enjoy music, or watch a good movie together. As in other areas of your home, these rooms should be arranged and organized to best serve the purposes you desire.

If you are fortunate enough to have both a living room and a family room, then you can make very specific decisions about the types of activities you want to encourage and discourage in each room. Since many homes and apartments do not have space for two rooms, I will cover aspects of both in this chapter. If you use one room as both a living and family room, you can incorporate ideas for both areas into that one room.

ESTABLISHING THE DIFFERENCES

Generally speaking, I see the purposes for the living and family rooms to be quite different and distinct. I see the living room as more adult-oriented, suitable for quieter activities such as entertaining guests, reading, and conversing. I see the family room as the busier, child- and activity-dominated room, suitable for noisier activities such as watching TV, playing games, romping, and so forth.

Let's begin this organizing project by designating the purposes for the living and family rooms. If you have one room that fulfills both functions, use both columns in the chart below.

Step One: Designate the Purposes of the Living and Family Rooms

Living Room
- [ ] conversation
- [ ] reading
- [ ] music practice
- [ ] company
- [ ] _____
- [ ] _____
- [ ] _____

Family Room
- [ ] TV viewing
- [ ] active play
- [ ] games
- [ ] family activities
- [ ] _____
- [ ] _____
- [ ] _____

One way to incorporate both living room and family room activities into one space is to use a loose schedule to help define the differences. For instance, children can practice piano and use the room for active play until dinner time. After dinner, quieter activities reign.

Step Two: Eliminate

Now that we've designated how these rooms will be used, here are some guidelines about what to eliminate.

Furniture. Furniture is supposed to enhance our lives and make us more comfortable. It can have exactly the opposite effect, however, if we overdo it. Too much or the wrong choice of furniture means more work in the following ways:

- More dusting, polishing, general upkeep
- More surfaces for people to lay down their packages, coats, books, briefcases
- More display space for knickknacks and decorative items (dust catchers)
- Less room for kids to play

For instance, many people automatically purchase a coffee table and end tables to go with their couch and loveseat. That's fine, if they serve a useful purpose, but are they useful for you? If the tables in your living room are only there to hold a lamp or display "coffee table" books, maybe they aren't needed. Don't waste money and time buying and maintaining them. Put the books on bookshelves and change to floor lamps. Tables are more useful in the family room, because eating is usually allowed there.

Work-related items. One thing we all look forward to is a break from our work. Even if we stop working, it's hard to enjoy the break if nagging reminders are all around us. Designate a home for your work-related items so that they don't find a hasty home in the living room. Establish a place to put away briefcases, paperwork, mending, laundry and the ironing board. (See appropriate chapters for advice.)

Knickknacks. You already know how I feel about the infamous knickknack. Below are some storage tips for them. Decide for yourself if they are worth the upkeep.

- If you have quite a few, store some in your box storage system and occasionally exchange them with those on display.
- If they are really precious to you, give them a special home. Rather than litter every surface, end table and shelf with your Hummels, purchase a curio cabinet to display and protect them. (This also cuts down on dusting.)

Newspapers. There is a sickness (I'm sure) that relates to the saving and stacking of newspapers and magazines. All appeals to logic seem to fall on the deaf ears of those who suffer from this mysterious illness. For people who think they will get around to reading these things *someday*, I have this very strong admonition: "Grow up!"

Could your life really be so empty that you plan to spend your

Bookcase Don'ts

- *Don't "decorate" a bookcase with plants, dolls, candles, figurines and so on.*
- *Don't lay books on their sides and stack.*
- *Don't arrange books according to height, but categorize by subject instead.*

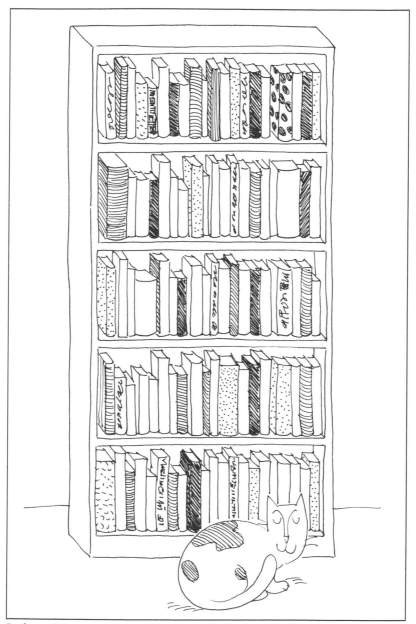

Bookcase Do's
- *Arrange books by subject.*
- *Leave no gaps.*

retirement reading the twenty-seven years' worth of newspapers — note that word "new" in newspapers — that are growing mold in your basement? Do you expect the earth to be thrown out of its orbit to the outer reaches of the solar system, where, by some mystery science cannot explain, our days will suddenly get longer? (What have you heard?) As you well know, newspapers are only good for one day. If reading the paper is important to you, plan enough time to read the whole thing and enjoy it. Resist skimming the paper with the intention of saving it for later. Later turns into next week. (Much longer, for some of you!)

Magazines. You are not fooling anyone with those back issues of *National Geographic*. They won't make you one iota more knowledgeable if you haven't taken the time to read them. And, if you haven't taken the time to read them, you're probably not going to be able to catch up (unless you're planning an extended vacation or some type of "accident" that will lay you up long term. What are you up to?) So, if you find yourself surrounded by magazines that are half read at best, then here are my suggestions:

> **What Your Helper Does**
> - Dusts living and family rooms.
> - Polishes furniture.
> - Waters plants.
> - Vacuums.
> - Does general pick-up and distributes stray items for their owners to put away.

- Cancel subscriptions to magazines you don't have time to read *now*. Don't save them for later. Your public library can probably provide you with back issues (or at least issues on microfilm) if you just have to find something.
- Rather than save a bulky magazine, clip the articles you are interested in and make files for them. (A large percentage of a magazine is advertising. Why hold on to that?)
- If you insist on being unreasonable and keep every magazine, then at least get them out of your way. Go to your local office supply store, purchase periodical storage boxes (see illustration), and store them in a dry location.
- Have separate racks for your magazines and your children's.

Books. Some view books as akin to the sacred scriptures — it would be unthinkable to part with any of them. While it's true that some books, such as reference books, are valuable to have around, others have served their purpose and should be passed on to be useful to someone else.

Don't fall into the trap of thinking, *I paid a lot of money for that book!* What you really paid for was the knowledge, skill or entertainment it contained. Once you have been educated or entertained, you've gotten your money's worth. (Compare it to going out to eat. It's expensive, you enjoy it, but you don't drag home the tablecloth, flatware and menu because you paid a lot of money for that meal. You don't have to spend extra time hanging around the lobby to "get your money's worth.")

To keep books that you have read and have no intention of rereading is silly. They take up valuable space, serve no useful purpose, collect dust and, like people, get old and crinkly. Do them a favor — keep them young, give them a reason to live, and recycle them. Your local library may be happy to receive donations. *Call* them.)

Tips

• Keep bookshelves and bookcases to a minimum. If you don't have many books, bookshelves are only an invitation to collect clutter. A vacancy screams for a resident. This makes dusting the shelves harder than necessary and creates a cluttered appearance.

• Store the majority of your books in one area of your house. (This is for you cowards who are afraid to live without them.)

• Categorize books. For instance, put all your classics on this shelf, chess books on that shelf, and mysteries on another.

• If you have more than two or three cookbooks, keep only the few that you refer to most often in the kitchen. Store the others with the other books.

• School books can be stored in your children's bedrooms or in the area where they study.

• At your office desk, keep a dictionary and a thesaurus.

GETTING AFTER IT

The first part of this chapter should give you an idea about the things you can eliminate. Once you have decided what goes, gather your sorting boxes and have at it.

Step Three: Containing — Setting Up Centers of Interest in the Family Room

In our three-step plan for organizing, we first designate the purposes of a space, then we eliminate things that no longer meet the designated purposes, and finally, we move to step three, containing what remains. In addition to corralling small items in containers within cupboards or drawers, this principle can include containing large items in an area or center. If you see your family room functioning as I described earlier, try to arrange various activity centers to accommodate the interests of your family. Refer back to your designated purposes list for ideas. Here are some suggestions:

TV center. With so many interesting things to do in life, I think watching TV pales greatly in comparison. On those rare occasions when there is something of interest to watch, we enjoy making an event of it. Here's a short list of items to include in your TV center.

• An entertainment center is particularly advisable if you have a VCR, tapes, and a stereo with its related paraphernalia. When purchasing, look for one that has enclosed storage to reduce visual clutter. For instance, doors that close to hide stereo equipment also conceal miles of cables and cords as well as stray CDs and albums that inevitably get left out. Having everything designated to one unit and concealed behind doors or in drawers is more efficient than having additional storage units for tapes, CDs, albums and so forth. It also requires a little less dusting and upkeep. As for tapes, contain them in drawers, baskets or boxes by category so that they won't get scattered everywhere.

• In a casual room, consider bean bag chairs or large floor pillows for comfortable seating.

• Afghans and throws are great to have on chilly nights.

Computer center. If your family shares a computer, the family room may be the only fair place to keep it. If you want to set up a computer center, here's a list of the things you will need:

• Special desks are designed to accommodate a computer with all its parts and paraphernalia. Of course, some are better than others, so shop around. Again, keep in mind plenty of enclosed storage. Look for a desk that will accommodate disks, paper, books and other accessories within its own cabinet or shelves. Whenever possible, eliminate any extra storage units, which get in the way.

- Some computer desks provide cabinet and drawer storage for disks, books and paper. If you don't have that option, store the paper in its box under the desk. Purchase disk storage units at a computer store and keep nonessential books with the others in your home.
- A clip-on light takes up little space and throws the right amount of light over your work area.
- Set up near a phone jack for modem and fax capabilities.

Reading center. The quieter atmosphere of the living room may be an appropriate location for a reading center. If you prefer to set one up in your family room, here are some tips:

- Comfy seating. A recliner or a chair with an ottoman is an inviting place to read (and doze off).
- Good lighting is necessary. A floor lamp with a small attached table can fulfill two functions — light and a place nearby for your tea.
- A magazine rack is one way to corral this month's issues as well as a stray book or newspaper.
- If you read aloud to your family, a few floor pillows nearby will help them get comfy.

Games/play area. If your family and children enjoy playing games, set up an area where they can have fun, but not where you will constantly be stepping on Monopoly houses and the like. Here are some ideas:

- If you have room, set up a table and chairs, even a child-sized set. Or, use a small area rug to mark the games area.
- Hang a swag light overhead to illuminate the immediate area.
- If you have lots of games and their boxes are falling apart, try this. Remove the contents of each box. The game boards are thin and can be folded and stacked together. For storing various playing pieces, dice, cards or money, you have a couple of options. Each can be bagged in a Ziploc bag or stored in a metal workshop cabinet with slide-out drawers, which are available at hardware stores. Another option is drawer and makeup organizers, both of which have several compartments. If you use the Ziploc bag method, keep the bags with pieces to a particular game in one container, such as a shoebox or

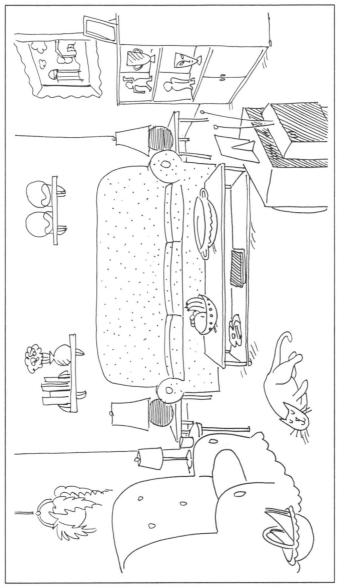

Here there are coffee and end tables cluttered with magazines, books, artwork, etc. The walls are cluttered with shelves whose only purpose is to shelve more clutter. Every surface is covered with knickknacks, figurines, candles, dishes, magazines, newspapers, books, vases, etc. There is too much "visual clutter" on the walls and in general.

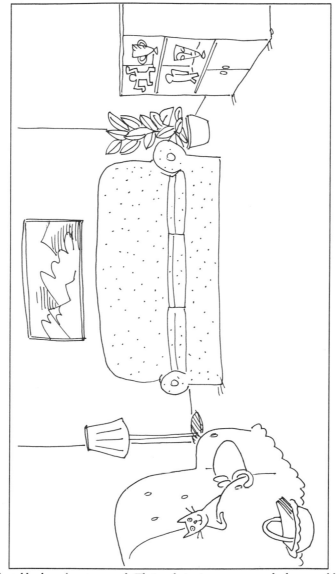

Here the tables have been removed. Their only purpose was to catch clutter and hold the lamps. A floor lamp replaces the table lamps. A lovely painting replaces the jumble of shelves, plaques, pictures, etc. A floor basket next to the chair catches the daily paper and a magazine or two. The figurines have been contained in one area—in the curio cabinet. This way they don't cause a cluttered look and they are also protected. The TV has been removed to the family room. There is now only one plant on the floor (in the corner).

basket. If you anticipate any problems, keep copies of the rules in a notebook close by.

• For general storage of toys, arts and crafts, and so forth, set up a mini-basket storage system in a cabinet or on modular bookshelves. The boxes or baskets can be labeled with the category of toys inside. (See chapter nine for children's bedrooms.) Whenever possible, enclosed storage is preferred.

Use this concept of creating activity centers to develop any other activity areas in your living and family rooms.

Puzzles. Puzzles should be coded as soon as they are purchased. Turn the pieces over and use a marker to code by color or symbol. Stack the trays together and store each puzzle's pieces in a Ziploc bag.

DECORATING

Naturally, we all have our own taste, so I won't tell you how to decorate. My advice is a guide to how *not* to decorate. By following a few guidelines, you can make your living areas attractive and comfortable without being cluttered.

Walls. Since walls are so big, most people want to cover them with various types of decorations. My suggestion is to limit the number of items that you hang. One beautiful painting, for example, is preferable to a variety of shelves, knickknacks and hangings. Not only will it greatly reduce the need for dusting, but it is a timeless item that will not go out of style.

Shelves. Shelves invite clutter and should be used sparingly. Use them for practical purposes such as book storage. Avoid using them to display figurines, plants, photos and such. They require a lot of upkeep but probably won't add that much to your enjoyment.

Photos. If you like to display family photos, I suggest you hang them rather than cover a shelf or table with the frames. This simple technique allows you to enjoy the display while reducing the upkeep.

Plants. Plants are lovely when they are healthy and well tended. If you choose easy-care plants, they are a wonderful way to add to your decor. My suggestions concerning plants are as follows:

• If you have children or pets, check with your nursery about plants that are safe to have in your home.

• Avoid floor plants, or at least avoid grouping them. If you have several bunched together, it makes vacuuming the area needlessly difficult.

• Rather than clutter tables or shelves with plants, consider hanging a cascading plant on a wall (but not so high that it is a bother to water).

As you choose decorations to enhance your home, consider the cost of upkeep. The most beautiful crystal vase looks beautiful only when it is clean. Dusting it every two or three days is a must. Remember, every time you decorate an end table or shelf with three or four unnecessary things, it means moving them when it's time to dust and polish. Try to decorate your flat surfaces so that there are only one or two things to move. Less to move also means less likelihood of accidental breakage. I recommend that everyone decorate according to the "less is more" motto: Less clutter is more conducive to cleanliness, comfort and congeniality.

As you arrange, organize and redecorate your living and family rooms, remember that it's all for a very good cause: the comfort of your family and the smooth functioning of your household. Good luck and have fun!

CHAPTER EIGHT

THE MASTER BEDROOM

HOW TO MAKE YOUR ONLY

HAVEN MORE RELAXING

*I*f you have a family, your bedroom may be your only haven. Away from the hustle and bustle of the rest of the house, your room should provide comfort and relaxation.

If your room is laden with miscellaneous clutter — laundry, tools, half-done projects, paperwork, piles of magazines — it can hardly be a haven. You owe it to yourself to get control of this room. Everyone needs a sanctuary.

TACKLING THE WHOLE ROOM

Depending on your situation, organizing your bedroom could be a big job. Please remember not to get overwhelmed with unrealistic goals. You'll be doing very well if you concentrate on one component a day. So, if you have lots of clothes and are very unorganized, don't expect to organize your dresser and your closet on the same day. Let's begin.

Step One: Designate the Purposes of the Master Bedroom

In addition to designating the general purposes of the space, I will also list the purposes of each component (dressers, closet) as we deal with them. The general purposes for the master bedroom are listed below:

- ☐ sleeping
- ☐ dressing
- ☐ grooming/makeup
- ☐ clothes storage
- ☐ romance
- ☐ _____
- ☐ _____
- ☐ _____

Step Two: Eliminate

Once you have determined the general purposes for your bedroom, gather your four sorting boxes and begin eliminating items that no longer meet the purposes. I recommend that, as much as possible, the master bedroom be kept free of extra furniture and work-related items. Let it be a room oriented to quiet activities, in keeping with the concept of a refuge.

Step Three: Contain

Start small and build your confidence. Do your own furniture and closet space first. Only do your spouse's if you want to and you have the OK.

Here are a few suggestions to help you get prepared. Because of space limitations, I will list them only once, but you should do this preparatory work before organizing each component. If you would like, check off the steps as you accomplish them.

Approach the components of a room the same way you would

approach the entire room. Always begin with the outside appearance of the room. In this case, make the bed, pick up items on the floor, and so forth.

Next, gather your tools: your designated purposes list, four sorting boxes, your list of need/want items, and cleaning supplies (dust rag, polish, etc.). If you want, set a start and stop time. Now lets move to the actual components for containing items.

NIGHTSTANDS
Step One: Designate

Nightstands should have a place for . . .

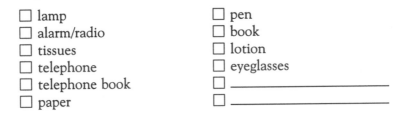

☐ lamp   ☐ pen
☐ alarm/radio   ☐ book
☐ tissues   ☐ lotion
☐ telephone   ☐ eyeglasses
☐ telephone book ☐ _____
☐ paper   ☐ _____

Step Two: Eliminate

Start by clearing out the nightstand's contents and its top. Then, do a quick but thorough job of cleaning. Finally, return only the items that now meet the designated purposes.

Step Three: Contain

Try to keep as much as possible contained within the nightstand's drawers or cabinet. Leave only the essentials on top. (Easier to clean, less visual clutter.)

Use the same principle you have been using throughout the rest of your home. Contain small items in trays or desk organizers. (Available at variety and specialty stores.) Or, look around the house for containers: margarine tubs, shoe or jewelry boxes, and so forth.

Sort the remaining items into your four boxes, and deal with them in the appropriate manner. Store the sorting boxes away at command central. Remember to fill out your need/want list as you work (small box to catch change, tray for pens and pencils). Finally, clean up!

ELIMINATING CLOTHES

I can hardly remember the reasons why I ever hung on to clothes so tenaciously. Of course, the old standbys, *It may come in handy someday* and *I paid good money for that* come to mind. Fortunately, I have become so adept in this area and have so far surpassed those excuses, I am never in danger of submitting to them again. That's where I want you to be, too.

Since you are now dealing with clothes, I suggest you keep a couple of extra boxes on hand. Designate them for seasonal clothing and items requiring mending. Keep a few safety pins on hand to mark the spots that need repair.

As you organize your dressers and closets, you will probably be faced with many clothes that can be eliminated. It's a lot simpler than we admit. Clothes either fit or they don't. We either like them or we don't. They are either in style or they are not. Whatever silly excuses you have for hanging on to clothes, rise above them.

If you find yourself reluctant to give up clothes that are not being worn, put them in your box storage system. Maybe after another year of nonuse, you will be able to part with them. You know, when there are so many people who can use decent clothes, it's selfish just to store them and let them go to waste. Think about it.

DRESSERS
Step One: Designate

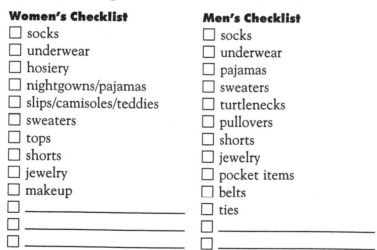

Women's Checklist
- [ ] socks
- [ ] underwear
- [ ] hosiery
- [ ] nightgowns/pajamas
- [ ] slips/camisoles/teddies
- [ ] sweaters
- [ ] tops
- [ ] shorts
- [ ] jewelry
- [ ] makeup
- [ ] _____
- [ ] _____
- [ ] _____

Men's Checklist
- [ ] socks
- [ ] underwear
- [ ] pajamas
- [ ] sweaters
- [ ] turtlenecks
- [ ] pullovers
- [ ] shorts
- [ ] jewelry
- [ ] pocket items
- [ ] belts
- [ ] ties
- [ ] _____
- [ ] _____

Step Two: Eliminate

Remove the contents of the drawers and clear off the top. Then, do a quick but thorough job of cleaning it. Put away the items that now meet the designated purposes on your list, and sort the remaining items into your four boxes.

Step Three: Contain

As you being to put items away in your dresser, consider these tips:

• Each drawer and cupboard should be assigned a purpose. If necessary, make a sketch of the dresser on a piece of paper and write assignments for each drawer. Work with your sketch until you are happy with the arrangement before you put things away in their new homes. If it would be helpful, write the name or category of an item on 3″ × 5″ cards and tape them to the inside of the appropriate drawers.

• Items that you use everyday should take precedence and be stored in the most convenient places; i.e., underwear should be in a top drawer where it is easy to get at and less frequently worn items, such as slips and camisoles, in a lower drawer.

• If you must double up items in one drawer, put things together that are always worn together, such as underwear in the same drawer as bras. Use baskets to keep them separated, or if your drawers are not deep enough to accommodate baskets, try using trays or shoe boxes instead. (By the way, don't fold your panties! What a waste of time. Just toss them into their basket.)

• If you wear costume jewelry, consider designating a drawer for that, rather than tossing it across the top of the dresser. The best thing I've found to corral earrings is ice cube trays. The compartments keep them contained, and it's easy to spot the pair you want. They're also great for chain necklaces and rings.

• When placing things on top of the dresser, keep in mind that fewer items make dusting and polishing easier. Limit decorative items, which quickly lose their appeal when they're not kept clean and tidy. As much as possible, keep items confined to drawers.

• As you return clothing items to your dresser, be choosy. Try to eliminate things that aren't being worn. To help your decision making, put questionable items through this test:

1. Does it fit? (*Almost* doesn't count.)
2. Do I still like and wear it?

3. Is it in good condition?
4. Does it need to be mended? (Put a safety pin in the location of the tear so you can find it easily when you're ready to mend.)
5. Is it part of a complete outfit? (Do you have a beautiful vest that you never wear because you don't have an appropriate blouse? If you decide it is worth keeping, start a box for items that need mates. Then, make a point of shopping for them.)
6. Is it appropriate for the current season? (If not, put it in the box storage system.)

• Be ruthless! Crowding your spaces with clothes you don't wear makes no sense.

Take care of the items in your boxes in the appropriate manner, and put the boxes away at command central. As you work, fill out your need/want list, keeping in mind items that can help you keep things organized:

- ice cube trays for jewelry
- desk-drawer organizers for jewelry
- baskets to separate items that share drawers
- a basket to separate good nylons from those worn only with pants. (Be sure to code the nylons with runs. Use a permanent ink marker and make a mark at the waistband.)

If you have the OK to organize your spouse's dresser, follow the same steps. It is best if your spouse is present to make decisions about keeping clothes, but if you're going to do it alone, be sure that you don't throw away anything. Just put questionable items in a box that they can sort through later. This will also be a big job, so schedule it for another day.

THE CLOSET

The closet is probably the biggest organizational challenge in the bedroom. By now, however, you have experience with smaller spaces, and you should have gained some knowledge and skill.

What makes the closet such a challenge is that it is home to a myriad of items with different purposes, shapes and sizes. The space needed to house a tie varies greatly from the needs of a pair of pants. Pants, in turn, require different space than shoes, and shoes have different needs than dresses. Add hats, skirts, belts, scarves, blouses and sweaters, and you have a relatively small space to fill all these needs. A standard closet with one rod and one shelf is a pitiful excuse as a home to all these items.

Naturally, customizing a closet with extra rods, shelves and cubbyholes to fit your specific needs is ideal. If this project is not feasible, you can imitate these features with store-bought organizational aids covered later in this chapter.

As you go through your closet, think of ways to make it more space efficient and less frustrating to use. This project will likely be a two-parter. This first part will help you designate your purposes and eliminate unnecessary and unused items from the space. This will help you make decisions on the organizational aids you will need. Jot those ideas down on your need/want list. Later, when you are armed with your various organizing tools, you can come back to a closet that contains only items worth keeping. It will be short work to put your organizing tools to work in their appropriate homes.

If you plan to have a custom closet treatment, you should still proceed with the organizing outline. This will help you designate your purposes, eliminate excess, and decide how you want to contain your belongings. Sketch your ideas on a pad of paper. Rework and redefine your ideas until you are satisfied.

Step One: Designate

Women's Checklist
- [ ] dresses
- [ ] skirts
- [ ] slacks
- [ ] blouses
- [ ] blazers
- [ ] hats — hall closet
- [ ] sweaters
- [ ] shoes
- [ ] boots — hall closet
- [ ] outerwear — hall closet
- [ ] scarves — hall closet
- [ ] belts

Men's Checklist
- [ ] suits
- [ ] slacks
- [ ] shirts
- [ ] sweaters
- [ ] sportcoats
- [ ] shoes
- [ ] boots
- [ ] belts
- [ ] neckties
- [ ] slippers
- [ ] outerwear
- [ ] pajamas

☐ slippers   ☐ robe
☐ slips   ☐ _____
☐ nightgowns   ☐ _____
☐ robe   ☐ _____
☐ _____   ☐ _____
☐ _____   ☐ _____

Step Two: Eliminate

Remove your clothing from the closet, and place items on the bed for observation. Then do a quick, but thorough job of cleaning the empty space. Put away clothing that meets the designated purposes on your list and has passed the tests earlier in this chapter.

The remaining items get sorted into the four boxes, disposed of in the appropriate manner or put away at command central. Record needed items on your need/want list.

Step Three: Contain

Here is a list of organizing products that can be purchased from most variety, discount stores and specialty shops.

Shoe organizers. There are floor racks with wire loops for holding shoes in place, hanging-pocket styles, and a hanging plastic-bag style with shelves, which zips closed. I prefer the hanging-pocket style over floor racks. It holds more and takes up less space. Also, floor racks make vacuuming more difficult. The zipper on the hanging-bag style makes it cumbersome to use. You may like this style, however, if you have formal shoes you seldom wear and want to protect.

Tie rack. Of the many inexpensive styles available, I like the type shaped like a hanger with oval-shaped holes for ties and belts. Choose the style that seems convenient for you. If you don't like it, give it away and try another one.

Belt holder. As with the tie racks, there are many products available. An alternative is to hammer small nails into the stud that your closet rod is attached to and hang your belts from their buckles.

Scarf organizer. The tie rack I mentioned above also works well for scarves. If you prefer, hang a few heavy plastic hooks to drape your scarfs over. Scarves on hooks are more likely to end up on the floor, however, when they are brushed against.

Baskets. For your small, miscellaneous items.

As I recommended with dressers, do your spouse's closet if you want to and have been given the OK.

Closet Tips

- Hang all items facing in the same direction.
- Use plastic hangers. (Won't bend easily; will last for years.)
- Keep only three or four extra hangers in the closet. Keep them together at one end.
- When you remove an item to wear, put the hanger at the end of the closet for easy retrieval later.
- When hanging items in your closet, categorize them. Put the skirts together, the blouses together, and so forth. You may even want to group them by color, as the department stores do.
- Use laundry baskets as hampers. If you have room, use several, and automatically sort clothes as they are taken off.
- Keep a stain stick handy in your laundry basket to catch stains before they set. (Do this only if there are no little ones living in or likely to visit the house.)
- Designate a laundry basket or box for items that are dry clean only.
- Have a box or basket for items that require mending.

OTHER ITEMS

Sometimes, the furniture or decorations that we think we'll love are the ones that prove to be a problem. The chair you thought would be perfect for reading in has become nothing more than a rest stop for clothes. The antique desk, where you imagined you'd keep up on correspondence, has turned into a catch-all for every type of clutter. Even the lovely basket of dried flowers meant to brighten up a corner has been piled under by miscellaneous junk.

Though lovely in their own right, these items can become more of a hindrance than a help. I suggest you remove them from the room (they go to command central). After you have organized your space, return them only if you believe you have things under control so that they will no longer cause problems.

THE BED

When my husband and I were newlyweds, we purchased a massive, king-sized canopy waterbed. We had wanted a waterbed, and I had always wanted a canopy bed. The thick, solid wood from which it was built ensured that it would outlive us.

At first, I felt somewhat like a princess, lounging in that bed. I found excuses to idle my hours away, sprawled across its wide, comfortable surfaces. I wrote letters in bed, I made phone calls in bed. If there was any way I could get a task accomplished from that bed, I found it.

It wasn't too long before I realized the second price of that bed: the price I was paying in maintaining it properly. As I mentioned, it was solid wood. It was also huge. (In fact, I've yet to see another bed that big. I think they quit making them like that.)

As you know, wood needs to be oiled. The more wood, the bigger the job. Oiling wood is not my idea of fun. Of course, there were also cabinets, shelves and those pretty tulip lamps. All these nooks and crannies made for plenty of dust collecting.

Then, there was the linen situation. The natural movement of the water made the sheets slip. I could never find a set of waterbed sheets that would stay tucked in. We tried all sorts of gimmicks with elastic straps and Velcro. It took my husband and me ten minutes to make the bed in the morning—heaving and hefting the mattress (Do you realize how much those things weigh when they're full of water?), adjusting the sheets just so, praying that this time they would stay. But they never did. We always awoke wrapped up like mummies. Mmmm. Comfy.

Eventually, this beautiful bed, which we thought we would have for a lifetime, began to represent excessive work, aggravation, and uncomfortable, restless nights.

Have you guessed the conclusion? That's right! The bed had to go. And what did we find to replace it? Well, nothing you would catch a princess sleeping in. We wound up buying a regular box spring and mattress. Nothing fancy. No headboard to spend hours dusting. No wood to oil. No mirrors to keep shining. Just a wonderful, comfy bed with sheets that don't slip. It takes less than two minutes to make it in the morning. No fuss, no bother. Now that's what I call real luxury.

Under the Bed

If you stash things under your bed, quit it. (I don't understand how anyone can get a decent night's sleep with miscellaneous junk and zillions of dust bunnies just a few inches away from their heads.) Most likely, anything that has been crammed under there is not worth keeping. If it were, it would have a more dignified home. If you insist that you need this space for storage, clear it out and organize it properly with the appropriate tools. Follow the steps we've been using throughout the book.

Be sure to measure the space between floor and frame so you can purchase suitable under-bed storage boxes. Think logically when deciding what to store there. This space is a likely candidate for seasonal clothing and seldom-used formal wear accessories, such as dressy shoes and evening bags.

Contain your storables in one or two large boxes that can be moved easily to allow cleaning. A dozen small boxes will prove cumbersome and make the thought of cleaning a dreaded one.

Now, have yourself a good night's sleep.

CHAPTER NINE

THE CHILDREN'S BEDROOMS

SHOULD YOU EVEN BOTHER

TRYING TO ORGANIZE KIDS?

YES — AND HERE'S

HOW!

*D*oes the exhortation "Clean your room!" fall on deaf ears around your house? Could it be that you are guilty of the despicable "Do as I say, not as I do!" style of parenting? If so, I want to let you in on something: That approach has *never* gone over well with children. Let's face it, even adults don't respect those who hide behind that infamous cliché. The bottom line is, if you want your children to be tidy and organized, you better set the proper example in your areas of the home.

If you wonder if you should even bother trying to organize your kids, let me point out that there are good reasons to teach your children solid organizational skills. Having this foundation prepares them for adulthood. Like any other personal asset, it's something they will carry with them through life and often find useful. Also, it may promote cooperation between siblings who share a room and among the family in general.

MAKING IT EASY FOR KIDS

As you approach the challenging, yet rewarding task of organizing your kids, remember that each one of your children is an individual and will have his or her own ideas about what to do. Unless they have been begging you to help them get organized (OK, you can get up off the floor now!), work on several of your own areas of the house before you approach your children about theirs. Perhaps, after they have seen the improved appearance and function of other rooms and noticed a general sense of reason and calm, they will be more anxious to make some improvements in their areas. (Well, it sounds plausible anyway.)

A WORD OF CAUTION

Please! Do not go into your children's rooms when they are not there and throw things away without their consent.

- It's not your right; those possessions are not yours.
- Children will resent you for it, and probably won't want to cooperate.
- It sets a bad example, showing a lack of respect for others' belongings.
- It denies your children the valuable lessons learned from making decisions. You want to help guide their decisions and you need to accept their choices.

WHAT DO YOU AND YOUR CHILD HOPE TO ACCOMPLISH?

- Arrange the room so that it is easy to clean and easy to keep clean.
- Provide a home for everything.
- Eliminate overkill (that is, get rid of the clutter).
- Create a comfortable, functional atmosphere.

Approach your child's room in the same way you have organized your own. You, the parent, must provide the necessary tools.

Step One: Designate

Here, as in every area of your home, use your three progressive steps for organizing. It's important to do this with your child (age appropriate) so he will see the logic behind the progression. Start by going over the list below to establish the general purposes for the room. Then, as you work with each item (dresser, closet, desk), designate the specific purposes for each, eliminate the excess, and contain what remains. Let's look at the general purposes:

☐ sleeping   ☐ playing
☐ storing clothes   ☐ a retreat
☐ dressing   ☐ _____
☐ doing homework/projects ☐ _____
☐ reading   ☐ _____
☐ being creative   ☐ _____

While you don't want the room to be so sterile that it is uninviting, keep in mind these general principles:

1. Have easy-care furnishings.
2. Keep to a minimum items on the bed.
3. Keep to a minimum dust-collecting decorations, such as statues and knickknacks.
4. Avoid open shelving, which invites clutter.
5. Have sufficient, age-appropriate storage space.

Step Two: Eliminate—To Keep or Not to Keep

Persuading your children to eliminate the clutter from their rooms may be difficult. A good way of helping them to understand organization and to set limits is to teach them the same principle that you now use: Keep only as much as you are willing to keep reasonably clean and organized. Ask them the same questions you ask yourself:

- Do you need/want it any more?
- Does it work/fit?
- Will you use it/wear it?
- Is it worth the upkeep?

Step Three: Contain

When things are overwhelming, quite often we avoid them. It's not surprising that children are the same way. That's why it is essential for us to do our part and make things as easy as possible for our children. We can't expect them to clean their rooms if we haven't given them the proper tools to accomplish that goal. Therefore, it is up to you as a parent to provide the storage they will need to be organized. Make their success more than a possibility; make it a probability. Now, let's look at the individual components.

THE BED

The bed is usually the largest item in the room. If the bed is unmade, the whole room looks messy. If the bed is made and tidy, the general appearance of the room is immediately improved.

If your children resist making the bed, look for reasons. Is the project too time-consuming and cumbersome? (Remember the story I related in the master bedroom chapter?) A bed shouldn't take older children more than a few minutes to make. Watch them make it, and if it takes too long, see what you can do to simplify things. If they know it only takes a few minutes, they may be less reluctant to make it. Here are some tips:

• The cover (spread or comforter) should be easy to use. A spread is probably easier than a comforter and dust ruffle. As mentioned, dust ruffles have a tendency to get caught under the mattress when the bed is being made.

• Avoid ruffles, pillow shams, stuffed animals, decorative pillows and anything else that makes it more time-consuming and difficult than necessary to make the bed. If you have a little girl who loves ruffles and doesn't mind the extra fuss, fine. If it's too much of a bother, change to a simpler system.

• Position the bed so that both sides are away from the wall.

• The headboard, if there is one, should be easy to care for. Avoid spindles, cubbyholes and shelves, all of which require lots of dusting.

DRESSERS

Dressers should be size- and age-appropriate, with low, wide dressers for smaller children, so they can reach all the drawers. As I have said throughout, try to have no-fuss furniture. Painted or Formica surfaces are preferable to wood, which requires polishing and oiling.

When sorting out your children's clothing, use the same criteria for keeping or discarding that you used with your own clothes. Refer to the test in Step Two, above.

Designating the Purposes of the Dresser

☐ shirts	☐ tops
☐ pants	☐ shorts
☐ socks	☐ sweaters
☐ underwear	☐ jewelry
☐ pajamas	☐ pocket items
☐ grooming supplies	☐ _____
☐ _____	☐ _____
☐ _____	☐ _____

When possible, store only one category of items per drawer. When grouping items, combine things that are used or worn together. Use baskets or trays to keep items separate. If helpful to your children, mark the appropriate category on a 3″ × 5″ card and tape it to the inside of the drawer.

THE DESK

In a child's room, a desk will do more than provide a space for study and schoolwork. It offers a place for correspondence, art and other projects and pastimes. A desk also needs to provide a place to store supplies.

As you organize the desk with your child, designate the purpose for each drawer. Here is a checklist to help you get started:

☐ school papers
☐ coloring books/crayons/paints
☐ stationery/envelopes/stamps
☐ pencils, erasers, miscellaneous supplies
☐ _____
☐ _____

Once you have eliminated items that no longer belong in the desk, use plastic baskets and desk drawer organizers to define specific homes for the things that remain, particularly the small things.

Dealing with paper. Many paper-related items are kept nicely organized if you give children a hanging file system of their own. If the desk doesn't have a file drawer, use a cardboard file box (available at office supply, stationery supply, and variety stores). Having their own files will make kids feel grown up and important. You can purchase rectangular file boxes that will hang letter-size files one way and legal the other. Consider making hanging files for these items:

- art creations
- construction/typing paper
- stationary supplies
- personal papers/letters
- coloring books
- financial items (savings account)
- schoolwork, tests

THE CLOSET

Approach your children's closets with the same careful thought you put into your own. Here are a few additional closet tips for your child's room:

- Adjust rods to an appropriate height. Add more if necessary.
- Install cubbyholes or use baskets to separate and contain items.
- Install hooks for coats, scarves, and so forth.
- Provide organizational aids such as hanging shoe bags and belt/tie holders.
- Store seldom-used or fragile items on a high shelf.

☐ pants	☐ jackets
☐ shoes	☐ tops
☐ coats	☐ scarves
☐ dresses	☐ hats
☐ sweaters	☐ belts
☐ boots	☐ school items
☐ toys	☐ _____

Once you have determined the things that will make the closet their home, you can begin to find containers or homes for them. (Refer to the illustration on page 93 for ideas.)

Here's a suggested closet arrangement for a child's closet.

TOYS

I understand parents who want to give their children everything. You love them so much, you want to give them anything that you think will make them happy. The question is, Do piles of toys really make them happy? Is it good for our children to equate happiness with a lot of material objects? If your home seems to be overrun by toys, I suggest you evaluate your habits and see what sort of example you are setting. Children aren't the only ones who get carried away with toys.

If it is difficult for your children to let go of toys, especially those they have outgrown, explain that there is only so much room for toys in your house, and they must be kept in that space. (This is one of the benefits of a designated storage area for toys.) If the space is full, there is no room for new toys to periodically be added.

If your children are willing to give some of their older toys to younger siblings or to charity, they can look forward to getting new toys. When they are ready to eliminate some toys, suggest:

Set up a "basket storage system" for toys to help your kids stay organized.
Baskets corral a myriad of small toys. Larger toys find a home on the adjustable shelves.
Children will find it easy to use and clean-up goes quickly.

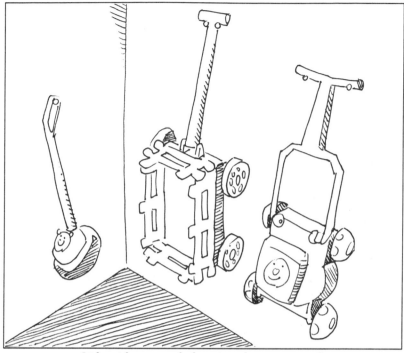

Lightweight toys can be hung in a closet or on a wall.

- Giving them to the needy.
- Having toy swap meets. This is something you could do with neighbors, friends and folks from church.

Toys that have been outgrown but younger siblings are not yet ready for can be stored in the box storage system.

Containing Toys

Since toys come in a variety of shapes and sizes, often with many pieces, they are a challenge to store. The ideal situation is to have a playroom where virtually all the toys in the home are kept. Most children, however, want to keep at least some of their toys in their rooms.

In general, I do not recommend toy boxes, because they are often too deep for children to reach into and because it's difficult to retrieve things on the bottom. (And, of course, it's always the thing on the bottom that they *must* have.) I think a toy box can be useful with certain limitations. It shouldn't be too deep, and it should be used for one category of toys. For instance, you might use it for balls and ball-related equipment — stow a football and helmet; a baseball, glove and bat; a soccer ball and knee pads; a volleyball; a basketball; etc.

Shelf storage. A better system for organizing toys is illustrated below. This is the system I use for my toddler, and it works well. The shelves are reachable, and the baskets are ideal for containing multi-piece toys. He can easily carry the baskets throughout the house (in his quest to follow mom), and clean-up is easy. He just tosses everything back into the basket, and it slips back on the shelf.

Some of the things you can keep contained this way include small cars and planes, blocks, crayons and coloring books, dolls, Play-Doh and accessories, letters and numbers, and action figures.

Self-contained toys, such as a farmhouse, are designated a home on another shelf. The companion pieces to the farmhouse are kept in a basket. I try to make logical themes for the shelves, whenever possible. The top shelf on the right is the "noisy" shelf. Here are the toys that make some sort of sound. The shelf below is "quiet." Below that are all types of balls.

If you like, label the shelves or baskets. For little ones who do not yet read, label the baskets with visual aids, such as a picture from the original packaging. I like this type of storage unit, because it is uncluttered looking and contains many toys in an easily accessible manner. Of course, not all toys lend themselves to this type of storage, but a large number of them will.

Larger toys. Toys such as wagons, lawnmowers and ride-on toys are more difficult to store. It's best if these can be kept in a playroom, family room or even a special toy closet. The key is to have a "parking" place for these toys. If they are very lightweight, you may be able to hang them from their handles on a section of wall or in a closet.

If you have a number of toys that you are constantly tripping over, you may want to house them in a cupboard or shelving system similar to that in the illustration. It may be difficult to find commercially made shelves that are deep enough. (I have been unable to locate any product that suits the purpose.) Of course, you could always build or contract for a customized system and several how-to books are available on building customized storage. (I particularly like Sunset books.) You may be able to modify their ideas to fit your needs.

If you have no choice but to park the large toys on the floor someplace, be sure to pick out a specific spot for each and let your children know this is its garage. After every playtime, that's where the toys need to go.

MAGAZINES

If your children have subscriptions to one or more magazines and want to keep every issue, here are several suggestions to help reduce the accumulation:

- Cut out articles that are of interest and keep them in a notebook or file. The rest of the magazine can then be recycled.
- Suggest they donate the magazines to a children's home or hospital or to their pediatrician's office.
- Take magazines to your children's homerooms, with their teachers' OK.
- Donate magazines to a preschool or day-care center.
- Offer them to friends or neighbors.
- Keep them in a "creative play" area as a source of pictures for artwork, for making books and other projects.

BULLETIN BOARD

I think most children like bulletin boards. Some of the items they may want to hang on one include:

- ☐ art creations
- ☐ report cards
- ☐ tests
- ☐ messages, letters
- ☐ blue ribbons
- ☐ school notices/lunch menus

As well as being fun for children, I think bulletin boards can be helpful. A bulletin board is a perfect tool for teaching children the three organizing steps.

It provides a *designated* place for displaying paperwork. Things of less importance have to be *eliminated* to make room for whatever is currently more important, since it is necessary to *contain* the items in the available space. As you can see, it is a good tool for learning how to set priorities.

ODDS AND ENDS

Here's a list of a few other things your children may need or desire, depending on their age:

- ☐ alarm/radio
- ☐ bookshelf
- ☐ calendar
- ☐ chore chart
- ☐ clip-on lamp
- ☐ hobby area/table
- ☐ keepsake box
- ☐ magazine rack

- ☐ mirror
- ☐ reading chair
- ☐ stationery/thank-you cards
- ☐ to do lists or appointment book
- ☐ wastebasket
- ☐ _____
- ☐ _____

GETTING INTO THE ROUTINE: KEEPING IT CLEAN

Once you and your child have gotten the room set up the way you want it, you should help your child establish a routine for keeping it that way. A little daily maintenance is easier than dealing with monthly neglect, so encourage your child to do simple things that will keep it up throughout the week. It may be helpful if you make up a simple, uncomplicated list for each child's room, outlining what is expected. Be fairly specific. For preschoolers who don't yet read, use little visual aids. Older teens may think a list is too babyish, so use your judgment.

The lists below are divided by time of day. For mornings, list only things children have time to do before they go to school.

Morning
- ☐ make bed
- ☐ straighten room
- ☐ personal hygiene
- ☐ get dressed
- ☐ gather lunch and school things

Evening
- ☐ homework
- ☐ family chores
- ☐ music practice
- ☐ toys away/clothes away
- ☐ straighten room
- ☐ wash up

Once a week, at a scheduled time, they could do a more thorough cleaning, such as straightening and organizing toys, dusting, vacuuming, changing bed linens, straightening drawers and closet, cleaning out files, and emptying the wastebasket. Again, if your children do basic maintenance during the week, this shouldn't be a big deal.

Be Reasonable

As a parent, it is your job to set the rules. You can require your children to keep their rooms tidy, but you need to be fair about it. Piles of clothes on the floor may not be acceptable, but I don't suggest you give them the "white glove" treatment, either. Yes, it's important to keep things neat, but there will be times (lots of them) when something even more important will prevail. I think that's OK, because that's life. Thank God there is more to life than keeping an immaculate house!

A WORD ABOUT DECORATING

It is my personal opinion that, just as parents are the king and queen of their castle, children should be the princes and princesses of their own rooms. To me, that means allowing them to express their individuality. If they want to hang posters on the walls or paint the room an unusual color, I think you should allow it (as long as they are not promoting something illegal or immoral). Allowing them to express their individuality and creativity is important to children. They will feel that you trust them and respect their feelings. If your teenage son wants to paint the room purple and hang twenty posters of Michael Jordan, what difference does it make? It may seem like a lot of visual overkill to you (and it will be), but if it makes him happy, so what? All his life, he will remember that you trusted him, respected his feelings, and gave him the freedom to create his own castle in your home.

Good luck with this project and remember: Taking the time to train your children and prepare them for life is *always* worth the effort.

CHAPTER TEN
MEAL PLANNING
MADE EASY

CREATING A ROTATING

MEAL PLAN THAT MAKES SHOPPING

AND COOKING A SNAP

*D*oes the familiar cry, "What's for dinner?" strike panic and shame into your very soul? Do you stand zombie-like in front of the refrigerator at quarter to five trying to decide between the frozen pot roast and the leftover party dip? (Are you sure that *is* party dip?) Do the people at your local fast-food restaurant call you by name and say things like, "Will it be the usual?" Well, if your family has never missed an opportunity to remind you that you are no Julia Child, let me give you hope: You don't have to be.

The simple solution to this whole pesky dinner problem is to create a rotating meal plan. This is a great system, and flexible enough that you can adjust it as needed to fit *your* family's needs. In fact, there are several reasons you might want to try some variation of this plan.

THE ROTATING MEAL PLAN

- You will no longer have to pretend that frozen waffles are a perfectly normal main dish.
- You (and your nosey family) will always know what's for dinner, even three Tuesdays from now.
- Once you establish your meal plan, you won't have to bother with it again, unless you want to.
- You'll be less likely to come home from the store with a bunch of ingredients, none of which combine to fit any one recipe. (I was great at that.)
- You will prepare meals you know your family will eat, as well as trying out interesting new recipes.

YOUR ASSIGNMENT, SHOULD YOU DECIDE TO ACCEPT IT . . .

Your goal is to establish a twenty-eight-day (4 weeks) evening meal plan. You may extend it if you like, but it's not necessary. With this plan, you will eat each meal only thirteen times in a year. Follow your plan for twenty-eight days, preparing a variety of meals, then when the twenty-eight days are up, start over. It's that easy!

If you have been preparing the same old thing over and over, this may seem like a herculean task to you. Don't allow yourself to become overwhelmed. It's fun. Take it in small bites. (Ha!) Work on establishing a one-week menu plan. That's easy enough. If necessary, repeat it as you try out recipes, and extend it into a four-week plan. And remember, once you have created your meal plan, you never have to wonder about dinner again.

WHERE DO I START?
Step One: Gather Your Recipes

Start with your tried and true recipes. These are your favorites, the ones you know your family likes and will eat. If you have enough for four weeks, skip ahead to the section on setting up the plan. If you haven't got many recipes or need ideas for more, continue on.

Step Two: Planning Meals Your Family Will Eat

(You don't have to be a magician!)

Have you ever slaved over what you thought was a wonderful meal, only to have it met by suspicious looks and disdainful comments? Of course you have.

Meal preparation, along with its related tasks of grocery shopping and clean up, is much too time-consuming and important to be troubled with such afflictions. The way to avoid them is to prepare meals that please your family and, therefore, you.

Spend a moment thinking about what objectives you want your meals to fulfill:

1. To be healthy, nutritious.
2. To taste good, so your family will eat it.
3. To be affordable, within your budget.
4. To require a reasonable amount of time and energy (not too much).
5. To be attractive, colorful, fun to eat.

It has been said that variety is the spice of life, so use a variety of main dishes each week:

- chicken
- fish
- ground beef
- pork
- beef
- nonmeat

We also know that attractiveness, color contrast and texture add to the appeal and success of a meal. Consider including some of these contrasts:

- hot-cold
- sweet-sour
- spicy-bland
- smooth-crunchy
- soft-chewy

This doesn't seem as intimidating when you think of a versatile food such as Jello. It alone fits four of the categories above. It's cold, soft, sweet and smooth. Add crunchy fruit or vegetables and you've got snap!

Don't underestimate the importance of color contrasts in your meal preparation. Before I got organized, I never knew what was for dinner until I grabbed something and started cooking. I got caught low on groceries several times. Baked cod with white rice doesn't do much to enhance a plate or an appetite. Bold color contrasts make a meal inviting and seem to stimulate the appetite.

GETTING THEIR INPUT

If you still feel uneasy about planning meals that your family will eat, do the logical thing: Go to the source. Ask each member of your family to suggest at least three to four main dish ideas. They may even be willing to suggest a side dish or two. Of course, you run the risk of getting responses like "s'mores."

Let your family know that you are serious and care about preparing meals they like. Remember, every night doesn't have to be a gourmet feast. Sometimes, the simplest things are actually what our families like best.

Step Three: Setting Up the Plan

Using the blank chart (page 104) and my sample meal plan (page 105) as a guide, begin to fill in your meal plan. (Use pencil.) Look over the tips below to make it easier. If it's helpful, you can duplicate my plan exactly using these tips. Later, as you gain confidence, change it as you like.

• Your first objective is to decide on your main dish. Don't worry too much about meeting each goal that we reviewed earlier. You can always work on improving each meal over time.

• Make notations about side dishes as you decide on your main dishes. If you are used to serving certain side dishes with a main dish, great. It's all the easier for you. If not, don't worry about it now. Plan simple side dishes for now and work your way to more elaborate ones later, if you'd like.

• Always make a note to yourself about the next night's meal. Remind yourself to remove the meat from the freezer, start a marinade, make a gelatin salad, and so forth. If you remove tomorrow

MONDAY	TUESDAY	WEDNESDAY	THURSDAY	FRIDAY	SATURDAY	SUNDAY

MONDAY	TUESDAY	WEDNESDAY	THURSDAY	FRIDAY	SATURDAY	SUNDAY
BEEF STROGANOFF GREEN BEANS W/ALMONDS ORANGE JELLO SALAD	PASTA SALAD PASTA SALAD BREAD STICKS	LEFTOVERS THAW HALIBUT	CHEESY HALIBUT BROCCOLI BEAN SALAD	PIZZA	NEW RECIPE THAW CHICKEN	CHICKEN CACCIATORE HOT VEGETABLE SALAD ROLLS THAW GR. BEEF
MEATLOAF SCALLOPED POTATOES TOSSED SALAD	VEGGIE STIR-FRY RICE ROLLS	LEFTOVERS THAW SHRIMP	STIRFRY SHRIMP W/RICE+VEGGIES BREAD THAW GR. BEEF	TACOS	NEW RECIPE THAW CHICKEN	CHICKEN BROCCOLI STIRFRY MASHED POTATOES ROLLS THAW STEW MEAT
BEEF STEW SCRATCH BISCUITS SALAD	MANICOTTI (RICOTTA + MOZZARELLA) ITALIAN BREAD GREEN SALAD	LEFTOVERS	PASTRY STUFFED SALMON RING DINNER SALAD SOUR CREAM THAW GR BEEF	GRILLED BURGERS	NEW RECIPE THAW CUT-UP CHICKEN	BBQ CHICKEN TOSSED GREEN SALAD POTATO SALAD THAW POT ROAST
POT ROAST CARROTS NEW POTATOES GREEN BEANS DINNER ROLLS	CHILI RELLENOS (EGG VERSION) SOPAS SCALLOPED VEGGIES	LEFTOVERS THAW FILLETS	FISH BAKE SALAD RED JELLO FRUIT SALAD BREAD STICKS THAW GR. BEEF	WONTONS	NEW RECIPE THAW CHICKEN	GINGERED CHICKEN RICE AVOCADO SALAD THAW BEEF MAKE JELLO

night's meat from the freezer at the start of tonight's meal preparation, it should have plenty of time to thaw in the refrigerator. Also, you won't have to worry about trying to remember to do it the next day.

MAKING IT EASY
Use these tips to make meal planning and preparation easy on yourself.

Choose Certain Nights for Certain Types of Meals
- Monday — Beef
- Tuesday — Nonmeat
- Wednesday — Leftovers
- Thursday — Fish
- Friday — Fun night
- Saturday — New recipes
- Sunday — Chicken

Choose a Specific Night to Be Leftovers Night
Choose a night that is normally hectic. Do you have a class, club meeting or church one night a week? Make that leftovers night. By making just a little more than usual of your other meals, you can have a mini-smorgasbord one night a week. Pop everything into the microwave and *presto*, an easy meal with lots of variety.

Choose a Night for Trying New Recipes
If you enjoy trying new recipes, I suggest you limit yourself to once a week at most. New recipes may require having ingredients on hand that are not staples in your kitchen, and therefore can be expensive. Also, trying something new usually requires more time and care. If you do want to experiment on a weekly basis, choose a night when you have extra time and energy. If you are usually pooped during the week, choose Saturday or Sunday for experimenting. If you like the meal well enough to keep, make a note of the preparation time for future reference.

Choose a Night for a Fun Dinner

After a hard week of work and school, your family might enjoy having one weekend night as "fun" night. This is the time to prepare pizza, burgers, tacos and hoagies.

Other Ideas for Specialty Nights

Here is a list of ideas for adding specialty dinners to your weekly calendar:

- Ethnic food night — Chinese, Italian, Mexican, etc.
- Dad's night to cook
- Teen's night to cook
- Eat-out night
- Sandwich night
- Salad night
- Anything else you can think of that your family would enjoy

If you are going to have a leftovers night as I suggest, reduce your total recipes from twenty-eight to twenty-four. If you also want to try a new recipe each week, you can reduce your recipes from twenty-four to twenty.

KEEPING TRACK OF YOUR RECIPES

To reduce confusion, it's a good idea to separate your *To Be Tried* (TBT) recipes from your *Tried and True* (TAT) recipes. Here is a convenient way of storing them.

For my TBT recipes, I use a pretty three-ring notebook especially designed for recipe storage. It has pocket pages labeled with various categories. If I come across an interesting recipe in the newspaper or a magazine, I tear it out and file it in the appropriate category until I want to try it. I won't take the time to make up a recipe card for it until after I have made it and decided if I want to include it in my meal plan. When a new recipe becomes a TAT recipe, rotate it into your plan by eliminating a dish that you are tired of or have not fully developed. When possible, trade it with another recipe of the same main dish category. Or, trade it with a less healthy choice — a new fish for an old ground beef.

For TAT meals, there are different systems for keeping track of

SYSTEM 1   *Front of card*   *Back of card*

MEATLOAF DINNER

MEATLOAF -   PILLSBURY
              p.127

SCALLOPED   BETTY
POTATOES   CROCKER
             p. 216

TOSSED SALAD

SHOPPING

MEATLOAF   V8
              DRY MUSTARD

SCALLOPED   MOZZARELLA
POTATOES   CHEESE

SYSTEM 2   *Front of card*   *Back of card*

RECIPES FOR: GROUND BEEF

MEXICAN SOUP   RECIPE BOX

CHILE RELLENOS   FRUGAL GOUR
#2   P. 37

WON TONS   MY OWN

MEAT LOAF   PILLSBURY
                 P.127

ENCHILADAS   BETTY CROCKER
                 P.647

SHOPPING

MEXICAN SOUP   GARBANZO B's
                CILANTRO

CHILI RELLENOS WHOLE GREEN
                CHILES - JACK
                CHEESE

WON TONS   TACO MIX

MEATLOAF   V8
                DRY MUSTARD

ENCHILADAS   GREEN OLIVES
                SPICY SAUCE

SYSTEM 3   *Front of card*   *Back of card*

ONE WEEK MENU PLAN

MON   SPAGHETTI   MY OWN

TUES   CHICKEN   MY OWN
       STIRFRY

WED   LEFTOVERS

THURS MEXICAN SOUP   (BOX)

FRI   PIZZA   SCRATCH

SAT   CHEEZY HALIBUT (BOX)

SUN   POT ROAST   BC #214

SHOPPING

SPAGHETTI -   FRENCH BREAD

CHICKEN -   GINGER

MEXICAN -   GARBANZO B's
SOUP   CILANTRO

PIZZA -   PEPPERONI

HALIBUT -   MOZZARELLA

ROAST -   ONION SOUP
              NEW POTATOES

your recipe cards. Look over the illustrations above and choose the one that seems most convenient.

1. Create a recipe card for each main dish. Make notes about side dishes. Put a star next to unusual grocery items. (Not illus-

PRODUCE	DAIRY	MEATS
leafy lettuce	skim milk	whole chicken
Roma tomatoes	eggs	2 lbs ground
avocado		beef
bananas		

SPICES
ginger
olive oil

CANNED
tomato soup

HEALTH
vitamins

DRY/BAGGED
pasta twirls
pinto beans
rice

UTILITY
napkins
paper towels
aluminum foil

HYGIENE
toothpaste
deodorant

FROZEN
grape juice
popsicles

BABY
diapers
bottle brush

NON-FOOD
movie
flowers
B-day card
for Jennifer

CLEANING
comet
sponges
veg. brush

PET
dog food

Organize your shopping list by categories, and post it
where everyone can add to it throughout the week.

trated.)

2. Make a card for each meal, but simply note which cookbook contains directions for each dish. Make a shopping list on the back of the card. (Illustrated as system 1.)
3. Make a card noting the recipes for a particular main dish group. Note where the recipes can be found and make shopping notes on the back of the card. (Illustrated as system 2.)
4. Using a large file card (4" × 6" or 5" × 7"), record your entire week's menus and where to find the recipes. Put your shopping list on the back. With this system you will have four cards, one for each week of the rotation. (Illustrated as system 3.)

Shopping Tips

• Keep your grocery list where your family can add to it throughout the week. Conspicuous places might be: on the inside of a cupboard door, on the side of the refrigerator, or on a bulletin board.

• When preparing your list, review your meal plan for the coming week. Use the shopping list on your recipe cards to add to it, or if you chose method number four, you could carry the card with you.

• If you have plenty of cupboard space and do not mind storing extra items, put a seldom-used item on your list as you use the last of it. Since this recipe won't rotate back for a few weeks, do this only if you have room. If you decide not to put it on your list right away, don't worry. You will catch it when you go through your cards for that particular week again in a few weeks.

• Once you have your entire four-week meal plan finished, you may want to create a master list to use for grocery shopping. List everything you buy. List the ingredients for your meals, as well as household cleaners, and so forth, by category. Make several copies of this list, which may be several pages long, to have on hand. When it's time to prepare your grocery list for the week, scan your master list and simply check off the items you want to purchase.

• Before you go shopping, take the opportunity to go through your fridge to wipe off shelves and throw away bits of food. When you arrive home, you can immediately put things away in a clean refrigerator.

• Use my shopping list at the end of the chapter (make several copies before you use it), or create one of your own.

FREEZER MEALS

Some people establish a cooking day in their schedule. It can be as often as once a week or as infrequently as once a month. It can even just be seasonal. Use this time to prepare main dish meals in large quantities to freeze for later use. Freeze-ahead meals are helpful when:

- You have an erratic schedule.
- You are particularly busy during certain seasons of the year.
- You are aware of an upcoming event, such as a hospitalization, or are expecting.
- You often have guests drop in.
- You just aren't crazy about cooking.

If you like the idea of having frozen meals on hand but would rather prepare them in small quantities, double your favorite recipes when you prepare them in accordance with your regular meal plan. By doing so, you save the preparation time when this meal rotates back on your meal plan. Make a notation on your recipe card or in your cookbook that this is a meal you will traditionally double.

Freezer Meal Tips

- I suggest you freeze only as much food as you will be likely to use in four to six weeks.
- Be sure to cool a cooked food before you freeze it.
- If possible, line your cooking container with lots of heavy duty foil, cook the item, cool it, then freeze it. Once frozen, remove the meal from the container so that it can be used for other purposes. When you are ready to use that meal, slip it back into that container.
- Label each item with contents, preparation date, due date, and number of servings.

YOUR MEAL-PLANNING HELPER

If you have a child or children you would like to include in the meal-planning process, it may be helpful to compile a simple list of the regular jobs you would like them to do. Post the list in a convenient, yet out-of-the-way location, such as the inside of a cabinet door. If you have several children, rotate this job as you do all the others.

Of course, some jobs are not appropriate for younger children. Use these ideas to get your children started. Encourage them to do the following:

- Make suggestions on recipes to try.
- Make suggestions on side dishes.
- Help write a shopping list.
- Help choose ingredients at the grocery store. (This is a good opportunity to teach children how to choose produce, select cuts of meat, and so forth.)
- Help bag grocery items in a convenient way for unpacking at home.
- Help with the actual meal preparation, based on age and ability. Wash vegetables, make salads, set and clear the table, wrap leftovers, load and empty the dishwasher.

Meal Preparation Tips

- Draw a basin of hot, sudsy water before you begin to cook. Soak and clean as you go.
- When possible, begin dinner preparations after breakfast. Make salads, casseroles, desserts, gelatin molds, and so forth. This means more free time with your family later.
- Everyone who is old enough should clear his place setting, rinse it and put it into the dishwasher. Have each person bring at least one other item to put away as well.
- Keep your table items close to the dining area. If that isn't practical, transport them on a tray or in a dishtub to save steps.

BREAKFAST AND LUNCH

If you like the rotating dinner plan and are feeling energetic, use the same concept for designing breakfast and lunch menus. You may not have as much variety (for instance, you may only be able to come up with two weeks' worth of breakfast ideas), but that's okay. If mornings are busy and hectic around your house, you may be better off stocking your breakfast cabinet with a variety of hot and cold cereals, breakfast bars and muffins and letting everybody fend for themselves. Whichever you decide, I wish you *bon apetit!*

CHAPTER ELEVEN

THE KITCHEN

ORGANIZING THE HEART OF

YOUR HOUSE INTO WORK

CENTERS — AND

COMFORT ZONES

*T*he kitchen is the heart of the home. For most families, it's also the hub of activity. It can be a wonderful place. A place to socialize with friends or try new recipes. A place to teach children cooking skills, and spend personal time with them. A place for you and your spouse to share your dreams over a steaming cup of coffee. A place filled with good smells, good food and love.

COZY VS. CLUTTERED

An unorganized kitchen can be just the opposite; a nightmare. A perpetual mess, it's too embarrassing a place to have a friend. It's too frustrating to try your hand at new dishes. Having never laid a foundation, you find it too difficult to include children there, and it's the last place you'd want to escape to for a quiet moment with your spouse. Far from being warm, cozy and inviting, it's a room you dread and hurry away from with a sigh of relief.

Whatever your situation, if your kitchen does not represent warmth and love, and thoughts of it do not evoke pleasant feelings, you can improve it.

Before we begin, I want to remind you that the kitchen is a very big job, and you shouldn't expect to have it revamped in one day. Take things one step and one component at a time, and you'll be doing fine.

Now, what do you want to accomplish here? Check off the appropriate items and list any other purposes you have.

Step One: Designate the Purposes

- ☐ meal prep and cooking
- ☐ store food
- ☐ store pots and pans
- ☐ store tableware
- ☐ store cooking utensils
- ☐ eat
- ☐ message center
- ☐ teach children cooking skills
- ☐ homework
- ☐ planning
- ☐ socialize
- ☐ _____
- ☐ _____

Keeping It Clean

Since one of the primary purposes of the kitchen is food preparation, it is essential that you keep the area clean. As you know, the easiest way to keep an area clean is to keep to a minimum the number of items that inhabit it. In the kitchen, it is especially important to eliminate unnecessary items and to be motion-minded (efficient) for the sake of cleanliness and sanity. In other words, you don't want to move seventeen things to clean the counter or to get the pot you need. Cleaning will be much easier (and more likely to get done) if things are efficiently arranged.

Since so much of a kitchen's clutter is visible on its many surfaces, let's begin in these areas. Remember, you overlook what you are used to looking over. Try to look at your kitchen with the critical eye of a potential home buyer. After you assess the outward appearance, do your eliminating. Now let's look at the individual components.

Refrigerator. Don't let the top of your refrigerator be used as a family dumping area. Designate a basket to avoid this problem. I have a small basket in one of my kitchen cupboards labeled "catch all." (This is my answer to the ever-popular junk drawer.) If we have an odd item that doesn't have a logical home, or if we are in a hurry, we toss it into this basket rather than shoving it into a drawer or leaving it in sight on the counter. The rule is that we must deal with each item when the basket gets full. It's never allowed to overflow, and we never use a second basket.

Avoid letting the front of your refrigerator be your message center (more on that later). Remove all notes and store them temporarily in a basket. (Make sure people get their messages.) Aside from the cluttered appearance that scraps of paper cause, it's also a nuisance. When the simple act of getting a glass of milk causes a drift of fluttery paper, it turns into ten minutes of picking things up and repositioning them. (Wimpy refrigerator magnets never seem to do the trick.) It's crazy to torture yourself like that.

If you have young artists in the family, make them feel appreciated by designating a special place to display their creations instead of using the refrigerator. Choose a spot on a kitchen or hall wall, or even in the family room, to hang a bulletin board.

The only things justified to hang on the sides of your refrigerator are your grocery list and, perhaps, your meal plan. If you have no better options, and it's convenient, hang a dishtowel from a magnetic hook.

Stove. Stoves look cluttered when pots are left on the burners. If you are short on cupboard space, reorganizing may solve that problem. Also, avoid lining up spices on the top. Heat can damage them and it discourages cleaning, since there's so much to move. (Keep salt and pepper on top, if you must.) One thing to keep handy is a spoon rest, if you use one.

Oven. If you like to keep a towel on the bar across your oven door, hang one dark towel there. I recommend a dark towel, because I think it's less likely to look worn and stained. If you can't find a dark kitchen towel, try a dark bathroom hand towel. That's what I use, and it's more absorbent. By the way, when purchasing an oven or any other appliance, avoid black. It's very difficult to keep clean. (Just who are the wizards that design these things, anyway?)

Sink. Keep only the necessities on the sink — perhaps liquid soap or pop-up wipies for sticky hands. Sponges, soap, scrub pads and your dish drainer should be kept handy, but out of sight. If you have absolutely no room to store the dish drainer, get rid of it and use a towel instead.

Counters. This is where the kitchen can easily get bogged down with clutter. A good rule of thumb is, the larger the family, the fewer the items that should make counters their home. In a large family, more people will be in and out, you will be cooking in larger quantities, and you will certainly need the space for preparations.

Since your counters are central to any kitchen task, they are of primary importance. Any objects that make their home on such a choice piece of real estate better be able to offer top payment. The payment is up to you, as landlord, and the fewer the counters, the higher the payment. Here's a story to illustrate what I mean.

A young couple had an espresso machine. A visiting friend remarked that she didn't know this couple liked the bitter brew. The woman replied that they didn't, but her mother-in-law, who was from Italy, did. They bought it so that she could have espresso during her visits. The friend asked how often the mother-in-law visited. The woman replied, "Once a year for two weeks."

A quick calculation shows that this couple put up with the espresso machine for the other fifty weeks of the year. Not only did it take up valuable space, but they had to clean it (all surfaces in the kitchen get greasy), work around it, and move it just to clean the counter. All they really had to do to alleviate the extra work was store it. This is exactly the sort of thing you want to get out of your way and store in your box storage system.

Another logical option is to ask the mother-in-law to bring hers along when she visits. This young couple had kind hearts, but they weren't thinking logically.

This business of not thinking logically is a mistake that many people make. They buy all sorts of kitchen gadgets thinking that they are doing themselves a favor. Unfortunately, once they get these things home, they have to find a home for them. Then, they seldom use the gadgets because, after all, just how often can you eat curly potatoes? Besides, you practically need a degree to get some of these gadgets clean. I want to scream each time I see one of these new fangled kitchen helpers advertised.

As you review the appearance of your kitchen counters, consider the items that work for you and serve you well. If coffee is a part of your daily life, then the coffee machine is paying its way. If, however, you seldom make cookies, perhaps the cookie jar should go. My suggestion is that an item should be used at least two to three times a week to earn its right to make the counter its home.

Personally, I'm much tougher. I have almost nothing on my counters. Oh sure, they used to be cluttered with seldom-used canisters, an empty cookie jar and plants. Luckily, I came to my senses and got rid of the stuff that was causing me work, but not working for me.

At this time, consider the things that typically make your kitchen counters their home. Determine whether they are good tenants paying their way, or squatters, cheating you. Check off and add anything you are willing to keep.

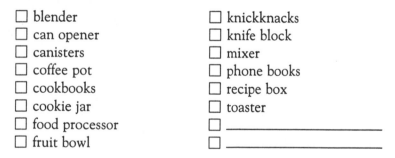

☐ blender	☐ knickknacks
☐ can opener	☐ knife block
☐ canisters	☐ mixer
☐ coffee pot	☐ phone books
☐ cookbooks	☐ recipe box
☐ cookie jar	☐ toaster
☐ food processor	☐ _____
☐ fruit bowl	☐ _____

Step Two: Eliminate

Once you have assessed the situation, you are ready to tackle the job of eliminating all this visual clutter and your infrequently used items.

Don't get bogged down by wondering if you should eliminate an item or put it in your box storage system. If you haven't used it in the last few months, but are still unwilling to give it up, ask yourself why you think you'll use it in the months ahead. Are you about to retire, so you'll have more time for dehydrating kiwis and making grilled triangle sandwiches? Are you expecting to get a maid so your time will be free to grow nuts and dry raisins for homemade trail mix? If you expect to have the same life, same job, and same schedule, please, do yourself a favor. Get rid of it.

Gather your four boxes and your need/want list, and begin. Proceed through the kitchen in an orderly fashion. Work with a plan. For instance, pick a spot to start, then work clockwise from that area. Or, work on each appliance, move to the counters, then the table, and any other areas in between. Remember to complete an entire area before moving on to the next.

Step Three: Contain

If you want to remove small appliances from your counter and store them in cupboards, but you don't have room, put them in your box storage system. Later, when you clear out your cupboards, you may find room for the items you prefer to keep close at hand.

INNER SPACE

At this point, you should see a substantial difference in the appearance of your kitchen. It should already be a cleaner, more efficient place to work. Just think, all this, and you haven't even started on the cupboards yet!

This brings us to the job you've probably been both dreading and anticipating: cleaning out and reorganizing your kitchen cabinets and drawers. These spaces are used to store and house many items. But what should you store and where?

Step One: Designate the Purposes of Your Cupboards and Drawers

My kitchen cupboards and drawers are used to store:

☐ food   ☐ place mats
☐ pots   ☐ spices
☐ dishes   ☐ baby items
☐ silverware   ☐ phone book/office supplies
☐ utensils   ☐ tools
☐ appliances   ☐ _____
☐ food wraps   ☐ _____

Once you have identified the items you want to store, you need to decide which drawers and cupboards are the most convenient for each item. Very few people have an ideal kitchen, so you may never be able to set up things as perfectly as you'd like. Just strive to do your best with what you've got. Remember that whatever method you try, it can always be changed. If you arrange things one way and find that it is not as convenient as you like, go ahead and try something else. To save yourself as much work as possible, consider all the changes you want to make before you do so. Careful planning can help prevent another change in the future.

SETTING UP WORK AREAS

To arrange the kitchen for its most efficient and most convenient operation, many experts encourage the establishment of work centers. There's nothing particularly mysterious about this concept. It simply means arranging things so that they are located where they are needed. You don't need hot mitts at the sink or fridge, you need them by the oven. And, you don't need a vegetable scrubber by the oven, you need it near the sink.

This is another example of a motion-minded plan. Why walk across the kitchen to get your spatula from the drawer next to the sink, when you need it by the stove and should keep it there? It would be wonderful, of course, if we all had cupboards and drawers this accommodating. Unfortunately, that's not always the case. Perhaps your only bank of drawers is next to the refrigerator (in which case, your kitchen was probably designed by the same genius who invented those black doors on ovens and dishwashers).

Since you won't always be able to store things at their ideal location, don't fret. Just work toward making your kitchen as convenient as it can be within its present layout and accommodations. Personally, I see no real harm in taking a few extra steps; most of us could use the exercise.

The major work centers are: the refrigerator, stove/oven and sink. These areas constitute your main working triangle. Most of your steps are made between these areas. All kitchens are equipped with these basic areas, regardless of their relationship to one another.

Other possible kitchen centers are:

- mixing and prep
- food storage

- tableware storage
- pot and pan storage
- microwave
- message center
- planning/office center

Now let's deal with specific centers.

Step Two: Eliminate

The refrigerator. We're back to the refrigerator, but this time we will work on organizing the inside. If you haven't straightened up the outside, do it now. Refer to page 115 for suggestions.

If your refrigerator is due to be cleaned out, remove its contents and give it a thorough cleaning. If you do not have counter space to remove all the items at once, clean it systematically shelf by shelf.

Tips

- Get rid of all UFOs (Unidentified Food Objects). I swear, they are more frightening than the real thing. How can two tablespoons of peas, an ounce of pot roast and a half-cup of potato salad all look the same after six weeks? Vow now on your hands and knees to use up leftovers regularly and to dispose of the rest promptly.
- Combine any item that you can; e.g., the six jars of mustard that have approximately two tablespoons in each.
- Before you return items, designate specific areas for food categories. Adjust your shelves as needed. Suggested areas are: dairy, beverages, sandwiches, vegetables, condiments, snacks, fruit, leftovers, thaw.
- Use baskets (baskets in the fridge? Yes!) to contain foods in a particular category; e.g., a basket for fruit or a basket for leftovers to see that they get used rather than buried. If the thought of using baskets seems strange, remember that newer refrigerators are made with various compartments to house categories of food. Think of your baskets as an extension of this concept. Use them the same way you use a meat-keeper compartment or vegetable bins.
- Be sure to use clear containers when storing food in your fridge. If you do not have enough, put them on your need/want list. Square and rectangular containers are more space efficient than round ones.

I suggest you find a brand that you like and work toward eliminating the odds and ends of other brands until you have enough of the kind you prefer. This makes finding the proper lid an easier task, too.

• Always clean out your fridge before you go grocery shopping. Same day. Record that as a permanent job on your schedule.

• Remove opened foods from their flimsy original containers. Store in a clear container or Ziploc bag.

• If making soups is on your meal plan, keep a container in your freezer for leftover vegetables and meats that are too small to use otherwise.

The stove/oven center. What will you need in this area? Anything regularly used for cooking and baking.

☐ hot mitts   ☐ knives
☐ pots and pans   ☐ cookie sheets/baking pans
☐ cooking spices — separate ☐ utensils
 these from baking spices, if
 you'd like

Divide according to their frequency of use (daily, often and occasional). Use drawer dividers to contain them and keep the daily ones in reach. Or, put utensils used daily in a container on the counter, those used often in the drawer, and those used occasionally in the box storage system.

The sink — washing and prep. Because the sink is used often throughout the day, you don't want to crowd the area. If, however, you have a drawer or cabinet nearby, you may find it convenient to keep these sink-related items handy.

☐ vegetable brush   ☐ dish soap
☐ liquid soap/hand lotion ☐ colander
☐ vegetable peeler   ☐ dishwasher detergent
☐ paper towels   ☐ recycling containers
☐ dish drainer   ☐ sponges
☐ cutting board   ☐ _____
☐ trash bags   ☐ _____

This list has quite a few items, and you may even have added a few of your own. The key is to eliminate what is not absolutely necessary. For instance, I use neither a vegetable brush or peeler. I use a paring knife, which I keep in my knife block by the stove.

I do not believe in dish drainers. If you don't have a dishwasher, save some room and use a towel to absorb the drainage.

Under-sink storage. I've noticed that in most homes the trash is kept under the sink. Naturally, I have to be different. I've always kept my trash in another cabinet. Thanks to our aforementioned kitchen design genius, there usually seems to be a rather narrow cabinet somewhere that isn't well-suited to anything else anyway. If you keep your trash in a cabinet, paint the interior with a semi-gloss paint. It makes cleaning easier, and I don't think it picks up the odors as readily as plain wood.

The only items I keep under the sink are recycling containers and a basket of trash bags. (It's true.) By the way, it's a good idea to cover the bottom of this cabinet with a large sheet of plastic or even some plastic garbage bags. If the sink leaks, this little trick helps curtail damage.

The dishwasher. If unloading the dishwasher is a chore that everyone dreads, then time it. In a well-organized kitchen, when there isn't much lollygagging, unloading a dishwasher should take less than two minutes. Now, how can anyone refuse to do such a quick job? Of course, young children will take longer.

• Use a cabinet above or alongside for dishes and napkins. Use the closest drawer for silverware or store in the cabinet with dishes.

• If you have hot water conflicts, run the dishwasher at night and empty it before you go to bed.

• When loading, separate the silverware into categories. This makes putting it away faster.

• If you keep a basin of hot, sudsy water in the sink while you are cooking and soak things as you go, they'll be ready for the dishwasher without much extra work.

Mixing/baking. The best location for this work station is between the sink and the oven, if possible. Here are some things you may want handy at this location:

☐ bowls	☐ cookie sheets
☐ cookbooks	☐ spatulas
☐ mixer	☐ casseroles
☐ recipe box	☐ measuring spoons

☐ food processor   ☐ baking spices
☐ baking pans   ☐ measuring cups
☐ blender   ☐ _____

• You may want to separate your cooking spices from your baking spices. Keep garlic and other seasonings at your stove/oven station. Keep cinnamon and nutmeg at your mixing/baking station.

• Use the priority concept (most frequently used, closest to hand) when storing spices, or store them alphabetically.

• Discard unused portions after one year. For those you use infrequently, use a marker to jot down the date of purchase on the label.

Cookbooks. Limit these to the books you actually use. If you use only one or two recipes from a book, copy them onto a recipe card and save yourself the storage space.

A Lesson in What Not to Do

I had a client who had a small kitchen with little storage space. She had one large cabinet jam-packed with cookbooks. My estimate is that she had at least three hundred books, many of which were paperbacks, in that cabinet. They were so tightly crammed that if she had attempted to pull one out, several others would have surely come with it.

She freely admitted that she never used these books. She kept them stored there because they were, after all, a kitchen item. Of course, she had so little cabinet space (because of the books) that her counters were littered with items that should have been in the cabinet.

Let's look at it this way: She had at least 300 cookbooks. There are only 365 days in a year. If you figure that her family ate out at least once a week (which they did), then we are pretty much looking at one cookbook per day, and that's if she used them (which she didn't). That's insane!

If this sounds too close to home, give away the books you don't use. Other options are to put them in your box storage system or shelve them with the main body of your books, getting one when you need it.

Recipe boxes and files. Since a recipe box is used often, it pays prime rent and may be kept on a convenient counter. Files and

Message Center Board

notebooks used for recipes should be kept out of sight in a cupboard or drawer.

Message center — avoid message area madness. This area can turn into a paper nightmare if you don't monitor it closely. Some things you may want handy:

- ☐ phone
- ☐ city phone book
- ☐ bulletin board
- ☐ personal phone book
- ☐ pen
- ☐ message notes (from office supply)
- ☐ paper
- ☐ _____
- ☐ _____

The message center should be set up as close to the phone as possible. Let the message center *be* the message center. Do not confuse things by trying to keep your grocery list, your children's schoolwork, and your "1001 nifty things to do with bread sacks" list here. By now, you should have places established for these items. (Lose the bread sacks.)

"COMMUNITY" BULLETIN BOARD				
MOM Sew Sue's costume- play Sat. night	DAD Golf tournament for charity 19th all day	MIKE school play 14th 7:00 PM	SCHOOL EVENTS - - - - BAKE SALE 10th PICTURES 30th	May
BILLY Billy's Softball game 10th 2:00 PM	SUSAN B-DAY 25th	JOSEPH FOOTBALL PRACTICE MTW 2:00-4:00	SPORTS - - - - SOCCER 22nd BAKE SALE 24th DINNER 31st	1 2 3 4 5 6 7 8 9 10 11 12 13 14 15 16 17 18 19 20 21 22 23 24 25 26 27 28 29 30 31
I want to go to the Zoo. Anyone want to come- Sat aft. ~ Sue	I'm SELLING CANDY for Boy Scouts. tell your friends! Billy	CHURCH BAKE SALE 13th MARRIAGE RETREAT 27th CHOIR (Sun) 27th	COMMUNITY THEATRE SCHEDULE - - - - • SECRET GARDEN 18th • DOROTHY! 31st • CATS JUNE 1st	CONCERT SCHEDULE JAZOO BB KING 19th INDIGO GIRLS 26th

Activity/Calendar Board

The message center should be your central place for recording incoming phone calls, communicating (on paper) with family members, and displaying emergency phone numbers.

Tips

• Divide the message center bulletin board so that family members have their own sections. Even little children will enjoy this. Leave them "I love you" messages. There should also be a spot for emergency numbers.

• If you value your calls, do not allow small children to answer the phone and take messages.

• Train older children in the proper and courteous use of the phone. Teach them how to take messages. This is important.

• If getting messages straight has been a problem at your house, try using the message notes that many offices use. These have boxes to check off and lines to fill in and are available at office supply stores.

• Treat everyone's messages with dignity and respect. Other people's messages are as important to them as yours are to you. Make sure your children have the same attitude.

• If there are numbers you call regularly, you might invest in a phone that has storage for often-used numbers. The redial feature is also helpful.

• Keep your personal phone file at the message center and add numbers as you get them, while you're on the phone.

• If you are a doodler, keep a pad of paper nearby for this purpose. Throw away the sheet when you finish the call. This may keep you from scribbling all over your city phone book.

• If possible, keep a small trash can near the message center. Encourage people to use it.

Community bulletin board. If you have a large family or are involved in many activities, set up a second center, a community bulletin board. This serves as a place to record special events, birthdays, appointments, functions and so forth. If it's convenient, put it in the same general area as the message center, but assign it a distinctly different role.

Schedule a time on your permanent weekly schedule to clear off your boards. Or, do it while chatting on the phone. If you keep up with this, there is no reason why it should take you more than five to ten minutes.

Planning center. Since you are becoming such a wonderfully organized person, you no doubt appreciate the importance of an appropriate place to do your planning. Let this center be a fun place. Prepare your meal plans there, add to your grocery list, write out your daily to do list, etc. Even if your planning center is only one shelf of a cabinet, get it organized, and do your work at the table. Some of the things to have at your planning center include:

☐ grocery list forms
☐ calculator
☐ paper and pen
☐ coupons
☐ copy of meal plan

☐ appointment book
☐ recipe box (nearby)
☐ to do list
☐ basic office supplies

FOOD STORAGE

Your rotating meal plan may help with organizing food storage, because you will probably be able to eliminate food odds and ends and, therefore, streamline the contents. If you have very limited storage, avoid stocking up. Or, use a couple of boxes in your box storage system as a pantry.

There are a couple of different ways to approach food storage. Do what is comfortable for you. Try both systems, if you'd like, then decide.

System One: Storing Similarly Packaged Foods

This system is advisable for a small kitchen with very limited storage space. You can make maximum use of your cupboard space by storing similarly packaged foods together. For instance, you may have one cabinet or shelf designated for canned foods, one for boxed foods, and so forth. Adjust your shelves if possible, then label them to indicate what goes where. Be specific. Here are some ideas:

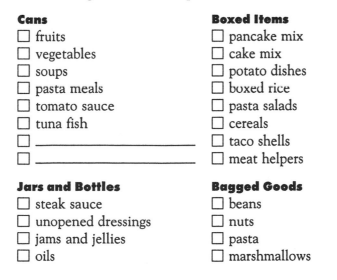

Cans
☐ fruits
☐ vegetables
☐ soups
☐ pasta meals
☐ tomato sauce
☐ tuna fish
☐ _____
☐ _____

Boxed Items
☐ pancake mix
☐ cake mix
☐ potato dishes
☐ boxed rice
☐ pasta salads
☐ cereals
☐ taco shells
☐ meat helpers

Jars and Bottles
☐ steak sauce
☐ unopened dressings
☐ jams and jellies
☐ oils

Bagged Goods
☐ beans
☐ nuts
☐ pasta
☐ marshmallows

Jars and Bottles
- [ ] sprays
- [ ] salsa
- [ ] BBQ sauce
- [ ] honey
- [ ] pickles
- [ ] _____

Bagged Goods
- [ ] rice
- [ ] chips
- [ ] dried fruits
- [ ] _____
- [ ] _____
- [ ] _____

You can even have a shelf for items that don't easily fit into the main categories.

System Two: Storing Food in Meal Categories

Designate a whole cupboard or shelf to each group. For instance, if you have school-age children, you will want breakfast foods to be stored in an easy-to-reach location so that your family can help themselves in the morning.

Breakfast Items
- [ ] cereals, hot/cold
- [ ] muffins
- [ ] pancake mix and syrup
- [ ] donuts/Danish pastries
- [ ] shakes
- [ ] granola bars
- [ ] Pop Tarts
- [ ] _____

Lunch Items
- [ ] soups
- [ ] chili
- [ ] pasta meals
- [ ] tuna
- [ ] bread/hoagie buns
- [ ] peanut butter and jelly
- [ ] chips
- [ ] _____

Dinner Items
- [ ] Hamburger Helper
- [ ] dinner rolls/burger buns
- [ ] potato dishes
- [ ] rice
- [ ] canned vegetables
- [ ] pasta salads
- [ ] _____
- [ ] _____
- [ ] _____

Snack Foods
- [ ] chips
- [ ] popcorn
- [ ] candy
- [ ] crackers
- [ ] Cheez Whiz
- [ ] fruit leather
- [ ] nuts
- [ ] hot chocolate
- [ ] _____

System One: *Similarly packaged foods stored together.*
System Two: *Foods stored together by meal category.*

Other categories you may want to create include:

Baby Items
- ☐ basket for bottles, brushes
- ☐ cereals
- ☐ jar foods
- ☐ formula
- ☐ bibs
- ☐ breast pump
- ☐ _____
- ☐ _____

Condiments and Spices
- ☐ teriyaki sauce
- ☐ Worcestershire sauce
- ☐ dry mustard
- ☐ oils
- ☐ vinegar
- ☐ pan spray
- ☐ salad dressing
- ☐ _____

Baking Items
- ☐ flour
- ☐ sugar
- ☐ mixes
- ☐ baking powder
- ☐ vanilla
- ☐ salt
- ☐ baking cups
- ☐ shortening
- ☐ molasses
- ☐ corn syrup
- ☐ baking chocolate/chips

Microwave Items
- ☐ popcorn
- ☐ cakes
- ☐ side dishes
- ☐ desserts
- ☐ packaged meals
- ☐ coffee
- ☐ containers
- ☐ paper plates
- ☐ _____
- ☐ _____
- ☐ _____

POT AND PAN STORAGE

Pots and their accompanying lids are like rabbits: They multiply while no one is watching. The problem, I have found, is that some of these pans are rarely, if ever, used. They simply take up space and drive everybody crazy. Think about it. What do you really need in the way of pots and pans?

- If you have a large family, you probably use a one-quart saucepan rarely. So, why do you keep it?
- Do you have to move the waffle iron, which you only use once a year, every time you want to get your roaster, which you use weekly? Why do you torture yourself this way? (You should see somebody.)
- Do you need that large electric fry pan, now that your family is grown and gone?

- How many burners do you have? That's how much you can cook at one time. Why not wash a pan when you're finished cooking with it, rather than grab for another? (You're going to have to wash it sometime, anyway.)
- Don't necessarily buy sets. Buy the specific pans you need to accommodate your meal plan.
- Store them according to priority, and put pots and pans that you seldom use in your box storage system.

TABLEWARE STORAGE

- Choose a cabinet close to the dishwasher and sink.
- If your helpers are young and short, choose a low (did she say "low"?) cabinet. Yes.
- If you do have children as helpers, use unbreakable dishes and tumblers. You want them to feel helpful, so why set them up for problems with breakable items?
- Work on creating uniformity with your dishes and glasses to make storage easier.
- If your cabinet is generous, it may be able to accommodate the silverware tray and napkins as well.

Step Three: Contain

Now that you understand the idea of work centers and have reviewed my suggestions for each area, begin to organize your kitchen.

First, make a sketch of each wall. You don't have to be an artist, just draw squares and rectangles to indicate where drawers and cabinets are in relation to the main centers — stove/oven, sink, and fridge. With pencil, jot down your ideas for coordinating various foods, pots and utensils with their most logical home. Note possible places for centers such as mixing/baking or microwave, if you plan to extend the idea.

Once you have your kitchen mapped this way, decide if you're ready to proceed immediately or if there are organizational aids you can purchase to help keep things contained. This containing principle is important, because no matter how well meaning you may be, things tend to move around if they are not corralled. Record your ideas on your need/want list.

One possible arrangement for tableware storage.

Tips

• Use drawer dividers. These inexpensive trays come in a variety of sizes that can be adapted for your purposes. Don't limit their use to utensils. Use them to separate bibs from aprons and keep garbage bags from lunch bags.

• Packages of taco seasoning, Kool-Aid, salad dressing and the like should be kept in a small basket or box. Even spices can be contained in a basket, rather than a dust-catching spice rack. It's no more difficult to pull out a basket of spices than to reach past several bottles for the one you want.

• When looking for containers, try to find styles that will contain a whole category of items. For instance, perhaps you use lots of sauces, seasonings and condiments at your house. Find a carousel large enough to accommodate them all so that half don't get shoved to the back of the cupboard and forgotten.

• If you are tired of pot lids scattered in every cupboard, give them their own drawer or pull-out basket. It's easier and more space efficient than keeping them with the pots. When you need one, there's only one place to look. Try this trick with your storage containers and their lids. I have a basket just for catching lids, and it's much easier than having them floating around. I save space by stacking the containers, and I can always find the proper lid without wasting a moment.

As for making the most of your cupboard space, there are many products available just waiting to help. Consider these possibilities:

- Roll-out wire baskets to contain everything from packaged foods to cleansers.
- Roll-out trash containers.
- Roll-out baskets specially designed for pot and lid storage.
- Tiered racks for containing different sizes of frying pans.
- Wire basket units that can be hung on the inside of cabinet doors to contain spices, packages, cans, and so forth. These are also available in full-size units for use in a pantry closet.
- Hinged racks that mount under cupboards and can be pulled down to reveal storage for cookbooks in use, spices, message center, knife rack.
- While many stores carry a variety of organizing products, they usually do not carry a company's full line. Any such company could have a product just right for your purposes, and you may not even know it. If you find a brand of products that you like, write to (or call) the company for their catalog. If the address is not on the box, call the library and ask the reference librarian. Libraries have special books that give addresses and telephone numbers of businesses all over the country. They should be able to give you the information you need.
- If you are hesitant to make the investment, consider that these organizers can be removed and taken with you when you move. They can also be a nice selling point if you opt to leave them.

If you find yourself lamenting that there just isn't enough room, no matter how organized you get, you will simply have to put everything that is not used frequently into your box storage system. Decide what is important to have on hand. If you need to have food close by, move more of your pots, casserole dishes and appliances to your box storage system. No excuses. You still have these things in your possession if you need them.

When you begin to empty and rearrange your cupboards and drawers, do so in an orderly fashion. If you empty everything at once, you'll only panic and invite a nervous breakdown. Let me give you some examples of how to proceed.

Let's say that you develop a more efficient location and system for your tableware storage. On your kitchen sketch, you designate the cupboard above the dishwasher to the left of the sink as the appropriate place. You have even designated particular shelves for particular items. For some reason, this cabinet currently contains packaged foods. Obviously, you will need to remove the foods. On your kitchen sketch, you should indicate where you intend to put them.

Now, if you have quite a few things to remove, you may want to put them in a box or basket or two. This way, you won't have dozens of odds and ends to clutter the counter and get in your way. Also, if something were to interrupt you, you could deal with one or two boxes much easier than all the loose items.

After you remove the food, wipe out the cabinet and install fresh shelf paper, if you choose. This will slow the process, so you may prefer to save it for another day, after your kitchen reorganization is complete.

You now have before you an empty cabinet. Before you start to put things away, try to think in a new way. It's easy to fall into old habits, but think instead about the most convenient arrangement. For instance, in most households you see all the dishes, bowls, dessert plates, cups and saucers stacked on the same shelf. This arrangement is fine if these things are regularly used together. However, most people don't use cups and saucers at each meal, so they could be stored in a secondary location, perhaps on the top shelf. If your family is constantly reaching for bowls, put them on an easy-to-reach shelf. What about drinking glasses? These usually get a workout in most homes and deserve a convenient location. Napkins get used at every meal, so keep them in a basket near your dishes. What about your flatware? Would it be convenient here? If not, designate a nearby drawer as home. If you have a set of dishes you use only for special occasions, get them out of your way and put them in the box storage

---

What Your Helper Does

If you have children who will be helping you, assign them kitchen duty for one week, rotating shifts. Here's what your helpers can do:

- Help with meal planning. They can choose new recipes for you to try.
- Help you compile the grocery list. Refer to your recipe cards and have them check quantities on hand.
- Check chore charts from other areas to find out what is needed. They can read bathroom charts to find you need soap and shampoo, for example.
- Accompany you to the grocery store. Help you pick out items. Keep track of the list. Teach your children how to choose produce, ripe fruit, cuts of meat and best buys. (If you don't know, ask the butcher, produce manager, and so forth. They should want to help.)
- Help put groceries away, learning about your storage system and organization as they go.
- Set the table.
- Be in charge of table clearing.
- Load/unload the dishwasher.
- Sweep the floor, wipe down counters.
- Put away ingredients as you are finished with them.
- Rinse off mixing bowls and utensils before putting them into the dishwasher.
- Help with meal preparation, depending on their age.
- Mix ingredients, knead dough, wash and tear lettuce.
- Measure ingredients in cups and spoons.
- Be the official taster.

---

system. There's just no logical reason to take up valuable space with them.

Once you are satisfied with your arrangements, make up 3" × 5" cards labeling the contents and attach them to the inside of the cupboard, adjacent to your newly organized shelves. Don't worry if the cabinet looks unusual this way. Who cares? Go for function and efficiency and forget preconceived notions.

When that cabinet is complete, you still have the boxes of food to put away. That is your next logical step. Store these items by using the same procedure. Remove items from the newly designated cabinet, store items temporarily in boxes, arrange the food as you like, label the doors. Continue with this system and things won't get too out of hand. Use your sketches for planning and strategy — they really help.

CHAPTER TWELVE

THE BATHROOM

TACKLING THE BIGGEST ORGANIZATIONAL

CHALLENGE IN THE

SMALLEST ROOM

OF THE

HOUSE

he bathroom is a little room with a big job. It is generally the smallest room in the house, yet it is used by everyone. Since it usually has very little storage space, it must be extremely efficient to serve us properly. So much is expected of this little space.

CALL IT THE CLEAN ROOM

When it comes to bathrooms, we want cleanliness. A dirty bathroom is a contradiction in terms. This is where people go to get clean. Good organization is the first step toward making cleanliness easy and to getting the maximum benefit from a small space. Let's get started.

Step One: Designate the Purposes of the Bathroom

The most common purposes of a bathroom are bathing and grooming. Below is a checklist of items usually stored here:

- ☐ medicines
- ☐ towels
- ☐ grooming supplies
- ☐ tub toys
- ☐ cleaning supplies
- ☐ _____
- ☐ _____
- ☐ _____

Since space is at a premium, store only those things that you really need to have on hand.

Step Two: Eliminate

Once you designate purposes for each bathroom, collect your four boxes and begin sorting. If you have any hesitation about eliminating an item, look below for encouragement. Remember, *less is more.* (*Less* clutter is *more* conducive to order and cleanliness.)

Sink and counter. The sink and counter area is where people do much of their washing and grooming; it needs to be clutter-free so that it is easy to use and clean. This space is more likely to stay clean if you make it as easy as possible to care for. To help cut clutter I suggest:

- Use liquid soap—it's neater and kids think it's fun.
- If you use water cups—have each child keep his or her own plastic cup in a personal caddy (more later). This also means less passage of germs.

Now, if you have any of the following on your bathroom sink or counters, eliminate them:

- Decorative soap—If it's not being used, it collects dust. Once it is used, it gets scummy. (That's not very decorative, is it?)
- Jars of creams, bottles of perfume, nail polish.
- Tissue boxes.

• Decorative hand towels — unless you don't mind if they are actually used.

• Hair dryer, curling iron — besides being in the way, they pose a danger here.

The only item I keep on my bathroom counter is liquid soap.

Beware of these other target areas for bathroom clutter:

Hampers. These collect more clothes on top of them than inside.

Toilet tanks. Keep these from falling prey to knickknacks, magazines, bottles, jars.

Shelves. Cute shelves that attract dust-catching clutter are an invitation to put it down rather than put it away.

Magazine racks. These store years' worth of *Reader's Digests* and never get cleaned out. (By the way, WWII is over. We won!)

Extra furniture. Any piece of furniture that is not specifically needed in this room will be a magnet for clutter.

Step Three: Contain

Now that you have removed the unnecessary items, you are ready to organize and contain what remains. Of course, you need to have a place to contain what remains. First, let's look at some ways to expand your bathroom storage, then we'll look at containing specific items.

Drawers. If you are fortunate enough to have drawers in your vanity, these can be given designated purposes and used for essentials. For an item to qualify as an essential, it must be used daily. Items such as toothpaste, toothbrushes, combs and shaving gear, for example. Use trays and baskets to divide and contain. (See the illustration on page 140.) Don't crowd this valuable space with less frequently used items like hair accessories, nail polish, or cleaning supplies.

Under sink storage. If you have a standard vanity cabinet, you can add shelves and use baskets as drawers. If that is not possible, use stackable baskets to create storage space. Also, you can use over-the-door hanging units (popular in kitchens) to help contain smaller items.

Wall storage. I like wall storage best, because the things you want

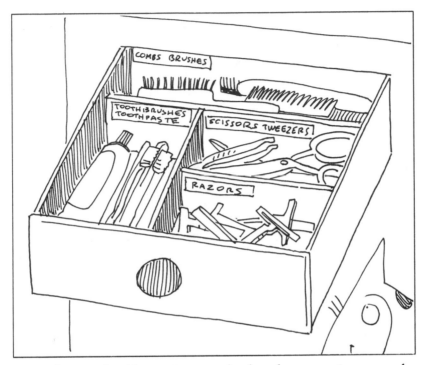

are within reach. Also, poisons and other dangerous items can be kept out of the reach of children.

In one home I lived in, all three bathrooms had pedestal sinks and wall cabinets. I loved the arrangement. With no counter tops to invite clutter, the bathrooms always looked tidy. The wall cabinets were wonderful. It was easy to get what you needed when you needed it. No bending, no pipes to fight your way past. It made so much sense.

If you are looking for a way to expand your bathroom storage, I highly recommend wall-storage cabinets. They come as standard units and as space-saving corner cabinets. If you are interested in something less expensive, check out the smaller, ready to hang versions available at bath shops and department stores.

Shelves. I do not encourage the use of open shelves, because they invite visual clutter. Use them if you have absolutely no other choices, and then only for self-contained essentials. Avoid using them for cosmetics, perfumes, nail polish, and decorative items.

Nonconventional storage. By using your imagination and good rummaging skills, you can create useful, attractive storage with items not automatically associated with the bathroom. For instance, a small chest of drawers can contain a variety of items. Even a small bookcase can be set up as a miniature basket storage system for the caddies.

If you are stuck for space, try an over-the-door hanging shoe bag for containing your hair dryer, hair spray, mousse, electric shaver and lotions. Another possibility is stacking bins, which are commonly used for vegetables. Each basket can be designated for a specific purpose — one for towels, another for grooming utensils and another for skin-care products. These items will create visual clutter, but, in a bind, go for function. Next, let's look at the individual items that need to be stored.

GROOMING SUPPLIES

If you are tired of cramming your limited storage space with the many grooming supplies and beauty potions that belong to your children, try this idea. Each child gets a basic set of grooming and hygiene supplies — soap, shampoo, toothpaste and so forth — and a basket to use as a bathroom caddy.

This is a good way to teach children responsibility for their own items. They can't very well complain that something was mistreated if they are the only one using it. It's also a way to minimize bickering among siblings about who used whose dryer, who left the cap off the toothpaste, etc.

If there is plenty of storage in the bathroom, the caddies can be stored there. The best idea, however, is for your children to keep their caddies in their own rooms. This minimizes the temptation for one sibling to use items from another's basket.

The caddies are convenient and carry everything needed for daily grooming. Everything is together, and your family won't waste time rummaging through cabinets and drawers searching for a misplaced item. The caddies hold:

- ☐ toothbrush/toothpaste
- ☐ shaving equipment
- ☐ floss/mouthwash
- ☐ shampoo/conditioner
- ☐ brush/comb

Short on storage? Use a hanging shoe bag in the bathroom to house bottles and jars.

☐ special cleanser
☐ deodorant
☐ _____

When a large family shares one bath, time is at a premium. In each bedroom, provide a mirror close to a plug, and let family members apply the finishing touches in their rooms.

A clock in the bathroom also helps people be more aware of the time they are spending there. If necessary, set a limit on the time spent (15 minutes max), so there are no problems getting everyone in and out in the morning.

When only one or two people share a bath, and there is sufficient room to store grooming supplies, simply use the basic principles — designate, eliminate and contain — to organize them.

TOWELS

While it's logical and convenient to store items close to their point of use, the bathroom does not usually lend itself to such common sense. If your linen closet is not in the bathroom, you probably don't have room to store your towels there. Most homes have hallway linen closets, so this is the logical location for towel storage. (Of course, you may first need to get rid of those cans of dried-up paint, battered toys and miscellaneous tools. Getting rid of the clutter means you'll actually be able to use your linen closet for its intended purpose.)

Limit your quantity of linens. Most likely, you do laundry at least once a week, so there's no need for excess quantities of towels and sheets. Go through them, and get rid of towels so worn they no longer absorb and mismatched sheets you never use. These items can be stored in your box storage system and used for rags, sewing projects, and so forth.

Towel Tips

• Limit or omit hand towels and washcloths if they are not used enough to justify their upkeep.

• Designate towels by color. Each adult and child gets their own color for instant recognition. Do the same with sheets.

• Use one towel per person each week. (Egads! One towel for an entire week? Okay, make it two towels.)

• Use round towel holders when several people share a bath. They work well and require a minimum of space.

• If you are in a real bind for space, mount a towel rack in an inconspicuous place in the bedrooms, such as on the back of a door. Then, each person can keep one or two towels in his room.

• If your laundry room is located close to the children's bath, have them toss damp towels into the dryer when they finish up in the morning. The person who is on bathroom duty for the week pushes the dryer button before he leaves for school. When the towels are dry, simply hang them back up. (This is a tip from a woman with a big family.)

MEDICINE AND FIRST AID

Because of the potential danger involving medicine, it is of the utmost importance that you *store and contain it properly*. Even if you do not have small children, friends or relatives may visit with theirs, and you will be more comfortable if these items are out of reach.

When my son was starting to crawl, I called the head of the local poison control office in my area for his recommendations. His advice was simple: Keep all medicines and external applications under lock and key.

Many parents are lulled into a false sense of security when storing medicines in chests above a bathroom sink or on high shelves in a linen closet. Since little children learn to climb and explore at an early age, storing things in this manner can't be counted on to protect them. Many tragedies can be avoided if parents take the time to store medicines and poisons properly.

And of course, common sense dictates that you never refer to medicine as *candy* or *yummy*, or use any enticing terms to persuade a child to take it. Also, because they love to mimic adults, never take your own medicine in front of them.

Once you determine a suitable location, keep all your family's medicines in that one location. It's safer for your family, and you will know what you have and what you need. You also won't have clutter in a half-dozen places.

Remember to carry the theme of eliminating into your medicine cabinet. Try to streamline the number of items you have, wherever possible. Be sure to check expiration dates and properly dispose of any expired medicines.

Now, separate your medicines into categories like these:

- internal
- external
- children's
- occasional
- everyday or frequent
- apparatus
- first aid

Having these items categorized and in containers helps, because it's easier to get one basket down from a shelf than to pull out several bottles and jars.

I use three categories to divide and contain my medicines — internal, external and children's. I also have a box for apparatus.

The medicines I keep on hand for my son are in a blue basket designated for children's medicines. By doing this, I am unlikely to grab a bottle of adult cough syrup or pain reliever mistakenly. Our adult medicines are separated by internal medicine and external medicines and applications.

Your baskets may contain the following things:

Internal
- ☐ vitamins
- ☐ aspirin
- ☐ Tylenol
- ☐ cold medicines
- ☐ throat lozenges
- ☐ laxatives
- ☐ _____
- ☐ _____

External
- ☐ Band-Aids
- ☐ hydrogen peroxide
- ☐ swabs/cotton balls
- ☐ Ace bandages
- ☐ thermometer
- ☐ rubbing alcohol
- ☐ sunscreens
- ☐ feminine products

Apparatuses
- ☐ hot water bottle
- ☐ ice pack
- ☐ heating pad
- ☐ vaporizer

Personally, I hate taking medicines. I prefer to keep only the bare essentials on hand. If you have quite a few medicines, however, you may want to add categories and separate those you use regularly from those you use occasionally. If you rarely use hot water bottles or heating pads, or have little storage space, put them in your box storage system.

First-aid boxes are handy to have around. They can be purchased at a pharmacy or you can make your own. Be sure to check on them regularly, so you'll know they are stocked when you need them. (Your family may get into them for Band-Aids and so forth.) This is the one thing that you may want to have in multiple locations if you have a large house or family. For example:

- In the kitchen for minor cuts and burns.
- Near an outside door for minor emergencies that occur while playing outdoors.
- In each automobile.

Use discretion when placing first-aid boxes in various locations. Keep them accessible, but out of the reach of young children.

I encourage everyone to take first-aid and CPR classes. *You just never know.*

Safety Tips for Storing Poisons in Your Home

- Keep all household cleaners and medicines in high cabinets, preferably locked and out of sight.
- Keep medicines and other household poisons in their original containers.
- Clean out your medicine cabinet at least three or four times a year, discarding expired medicines and those without proper labels, complete instructions, and so forth.
- Ask for items in childproof containers.
- Use Mr. Yuk stickers (a frowny face), available at poison control centers and some pharmacies, on medicines as well as household cleansers to warn of poison. Make sure kids understand.
- Put the number of the poison control center by each telephone.
- Keep syrup of ipecac on hand. Know when to use it and when *not* to use it. Do not use it on babies nine months of age or younger without explicit direction from your physician.

- To reduce a child's curiosity, contain several small bottles of medicine in a covered, wide-mouth container. Store this in your medicine basket.
- Ask your local poison control center to recommend helpful literature on accidental poisoning. Read and be prepared in the event of an emergency.

CLEANSERS

How often do you deep clean your bathroom? If you do it once a week, there's really no sense in using your limited space to store a bucket and cleansers. If there are children in your home, I suggest you follow the same theme as with storing medicines. Keep all your cleansers in one central location. I keep mine (and I only use a few things) in my laundry room. It's better to walk a few extra steps to get your cleaning products than to have the constant threat of danger because they are easily accessible to children.

In the bathroom, as in every area of your home, you should eliminate as much as possible. I have seen cupboards and cabinets so full of cleansers, you'd think the family was living in an operating room under sterile conditions. Unfortunately, this seems to be the trend in dirtier homes. Just buying this stuff isn't enough, you know. You've got to use it once in a while. Here's what I suggest:

- Avoid storing cleaning supplies with personal cleansers such as soaps and shampoos.
- Store cleaning supplies in a central location out of the reach of children.
- Limit the number of cleaning supplies you use. You needn't single-handedly make manufacturers and their paid advertisers rich.
- Use a shower caddy to hold personal cleansers used in the shower.
- Store duplicate products in the box storage system. Avoid buying too much. There will be other sales.
- Mount a paper-towel rack inside your vanity. Use the paper towels to wipe the sink, counter and mirror.

A Word About Cleaning

What supplies are necessary to keep the bathroom clean? Actually, very few. I use Comet for scrubbing the tub, toilet and sink. I use Windex to clean the mirror and chrome. I use Vanish toilet drops in the tank. And, I usually mop with a mild dishwashing detergent. If I want the floor to shine (which I almost never worry about), I use Mop and Glo. I've tried different products, but I prefer these.

Tub Toys

For safety, tub toys should be removed from the tub after each bath and contained in a net bag or plastic basket. Designate a storage place for these toys when they're not in use. If there is no practical space in the bathroom, then keep them in the child's bedroom.

DAILY UPKEEP

To keep the bathroom in order on a daily basis, each person in your family should develop the following habits:

- Rinse the tub after showering or bathing.
- Leave the bar of soap in the same, safe place. A shower caddy is helpful for this.
- Put personal grooming supplies back into their caddies, which are then returned to their bedrooms.
- Rinse the sink of toothpaste, and towel dry the counter area for the next person.
- Wipe the mirror clean.
- Refill the toilet paper when necessary.
- Properly dispose of wet towels.
- Wipe up water puddles on the floor.

All of this should only take a few minutes.

Go over this list with each of your children to make sure they understand what is expected. Check up on them for a few weeks to make sure that it does, in fact, become routine. In the long run, it will pay.

BATHROOM DUTY

If you intend to have family members help with weekly deep cleaning, I have these suggestions:

- Post a daily and weekly job list inside a cabinet, so the person or persons on bathroom duty know exactly what needs to be done.

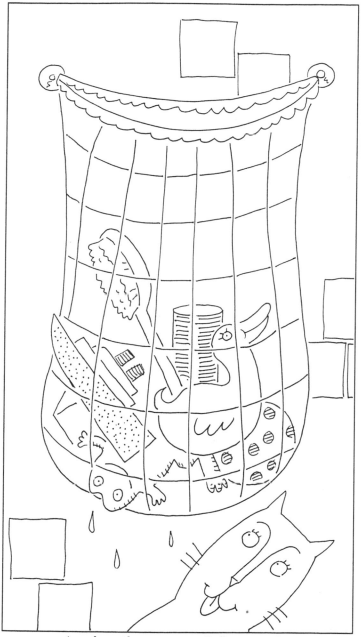

A net bag with suction cups will allow toys to dry,
as well as keep them up and out of your way.

BATHROOM CLEANING CHART

Scrub sink and chrome	Scrub tub and shower door	Scrub toilet bowl	under seat	under lid	base	Wipe down counters and shelves	Clean mirror	Shake or vacuum rugs	Sweep, then mop floor	Check cleaning supplies	Check grooming supplies

This way, they can't use the excuse, "I didn't know I was supposed to scrub the toilet."

• The person on bathroom duty is responsible for noting items such as soap, toilet paper, and cleanser before they run out. Have a place on the cleaning chart to jot these items down. Put up a velcro pen holder so they can check off their chart and list needed items.

• Don't assign bathroom duty (or any other chore, for that matter) to a child until you have taken time to clean with them and set the example. Don't expect them to see what needs to be done. Also, direct each child on how much cleanser is used, how to use it properly, how to store it properly, and when it's appropriate to list items that need to be replenished.

Bathroom Safety Tips

• Appliances should never be used in the presence of little children, who like to imitate adults and older siblings. They can hurt themselves by turning on a curling iron or dryer, or by imitating dad by shaving.

• Never allow one child to operate an appliance when another is in the tub.

• If there are small children or pets in the home, insist that everyone keep the toilet lid down.

CHAPTER THIRTEEN

THE LAUNDRY ROOM

HOW TO CUT THE WORK OF

CLEANING CLOTHES

BY A THIRD

*L*aundry is one of the biggest and most important household jobs. I rank it second only to meal preparation. We do ourselves a tremendous favor by getting this area organized, especially considering we handle each piece of laundry eight to nine times, start to finish. Don't believe me? Here's what it takes:

1. Put laundry in the hamper.
2. Bring it to the laundry room.
3. Sort it.
4. Presoak, if necessary.
5. Load the washer.

6. Load the dryer.
7. Hang or fold clean laundry.
8. Iron, if necessary.
9. Put everything away.

Being disorganized causes far more work than carrying out a well-planned laundry routine. In fact, you may be able to eliminate three or more steps if you follow my advice.

WHERE DO YOU START?

There are actually two phases to getting your laundry organized. We need to organize the laundry procedure as well as the laundry room itself. First, let's get the laundry room set up efficiently so that it can give us the maximum help. Ideally, this is a specific room for all laundry-related tasks. However, few of us have homes geared toward the organizational ideal. If your laundry room is shared with a bathroom or is simply a small corner of the garage, don't worry. Think creatively, and do the best you can to adopt the following ideas.

Step One: Designate the Purposes
☐ wash clothes
☐ dry clothes
☐ mend
☐ presoak
☐ store dirty/clean clothes
☐ fold clothes
☐ hang clothes
☐ store individual clothes baskets
☐ iron

To aid in accomplishing your purposes, a few helpful items to have are:

☐ a wastebasket
☐ catch-all for odds and ends
☐ container for change
☐ storage for cleaners
☐ permanent ink markers

☐ lint brush
☐ sponge or paper towels/ cleaner
☐ a shopping list
☐ _____

Note: If your laundry room is also a utility room, you may want to include such things as a place for tools, broom, bucket, mop, etc.

Step Two: Eliminate

Once you have designated the purposes for your laundry room, take your four boxes and eliminate anything that does not meet these criteria. Work on your boxes at command central, as previously discussed.

Step Three: Contain

Now that you have eliminated all the unnecessary items from the laundry room, you can begin to gather and organize the tools that will help you do the laundry job. Let's look at the items on our designated purposes list as they occur in the laundering process. You may not want to use every suggestion, but keep track of those you want to try by making a check mark next to them.

Mending

When it comes to mending, we have five basic choices:

1. Mend it now.
2. Mend it later at a designated time.
3. Have someone else mend it (for a fee).
4. Don't mend it — live with it.
5. Don't mend it — give it away or throw it away.

Decide whether or not you are willing to do the mending. If you are like I was and dread mending, you may find it a more palatable job if you use my organizing ideas to make it easier. If your mending has accumulated (I know you have piles!), it may be wise to take it to a professional so that you can start with a clean slate. If you can't afford to take it all at once, take a few things each week until you get caught up.

Schedule a time for mending. Just like any other job, mending should be planned. Look over your schedule and find an appropriate time to write it in. The size of your family and your past experience will dictate how much time you need to spend. If you make this a regular part of your weekly work schedule, you can stay on top of it, and it shouldn't require an inordinate amount of time. Also, you may find that you won't have mending to do every single week. Use the time scheduled for something else.

Put a small sewing kit in your laundry room. This is the simplest and most helpful way to avoid putting off spot mending that I have found. You'll be much more likely to do something about that loose button or small tear you just noticed if the supplies you need are on hand. The repair will take you just a few moments, then and there. If you have to go in search of a needle and thread, you may end up throwing the item back into the dirty clothes pile.

Small sewing kits can be purchased at dime stores. You can make your own by putting a few basic thread colors, a needle or two, a small pair of scissors, a few safety pins and a thimble, if you use one, in a basket. (Even a margarine tub works.)

Have your sewing machine set up and ready to go. If you are fortunate enough to have a large laundry room, consider using it for a sewing room as well. If not, try to keep your machine ready to go in another room. Have a well-stocked bobbin case with basic colors and with those in your wardrobe. Keep the matching spools of thread close by. I found that when I set up my machine like this, I did more hemming, mending, and so forth than I did when I kept it stored in the closet.

Choose a place and container for items requiring mending. Decide where the mending should be kept. An item needing mending is less likely to be overlooked if there is a designated place to put it, such as:

- Box in your closet.
- Box in the laundry area.
- Box at your sewing station.
- Box in each of the children's closets. You should instruct them to take these items to the box at your sewing area when they bring their dirty clothes to the laundry room.

Have your children help with mending. If your children are old enough to take on this responsibility, their help will be a great asset. It will reduce your work, and family members may be easier on their clothes if they know they will be doing some of the repair work. Besides, everyone needs to know the basics.

Presoaking

This may or may not be a regular necessity in your home.

Keep a stain stick in each bedroom. If you find that your children often have unreported stains, keep a stain stick in each child's room. Encourage your children to wipe the stain when they take off their clothes. (*Caution:* This is not appropriate if there are young children in the house. Tiny ones tend to eat everything.)

Use a brand of presoak that can be applied directly. Applying presoak directly to the stained garment is much easier than working with powdered products. If you prefer using a powdered presoak, you will need water and a container such as a dishtub for soaking. If you have no sink in your laundry room, transport water in your dishtub.

Presoak stained clothing the night before you do laundry. The key to presoaking is to catch the stain in time and to have enough time to treat it before the garment is tossed into the wash. To treat your clothes overnight, search for stained clothing the evening before laundry day, and use a product that allows long presoak times.

Sorting Dirty Clothes

Give everyone in the house laundry baskets. Rather than face several hampers of unsorted clothes on laundry day, give everyone in the house a few laundry baskets (boxes like the ones used in your box storage system will work) to keep in their closets. Teach them how you like the laundry sorted, and let them do so as they undress at night. This small change in your family's routine can save you a lot of time and trouble.

Have family members bring their laundry on the appropriate day. (More about this later.) To be sure everyone understands when to bring certain items, post a schedule in the room.

Storage for Cleaning Products

Enclosed wall cabinets. These are ideal for storing cleaning products and accessories since the doors eliminate visual clutter. If you cannot have cabinets, install a shelf. Avoid using the top of your machine for storage.

Limit the cleaning products you use. Don't fall for gimmicks. If you try a new product and find you do not care for it, either give it away or throw it away. Reluctance to do so makes no sense. If it sits on your shelf unused for four years, you still won't have gotten your money's worth.

Arrange your cleaning products in the order they will be used. This helps anyone else doing laundry by simply providing a logical progression: presoak, bleach, detergent, liquid fabric softener, dryer softener.

Label the shelves or the inside of cabinet doors. Once you have things in the order you want, label everything. This helps everything get back to its home.

Folding Area

A counter is ideal. This gives you the surface space for sorting and folding clothes the moment they come out of the dryer. If you don't have a counter, but think you have room to install one, consider the counters with Formica tops that can be purchased at building supply stores. If you want to use less space, you may be able to install a counter with hinges that folds against the wall when not in use.

Use your bed for folding clothes. If no counter space is available, this is preferable to the dining table.

Hanging

Use a bar for hanging. This is a simple and inexpensive technique that helps the whole process run smoothly. A standard closet rod can be cut to fit your laundry room. (Be sure to purchase rod holders.) As clothes come out of the dryer, they can be hung immediately to avoid excessive wrinkling.

Use a spring-tension rod. If you are unable to install a permanent rod, put one up as needed. When you are finished, take it down and stand it in a corner. Even if you plan to iron, hanging clothes is preferable to throwing them in a laundry basket. Use hooks if it's your only option.

Individual Clothes Baskets

Use the same laundry baskets to sort clean clothes. This may particularly appeal to someone with a large family. If you want everyone to be responsible for picking up and putting away their clean clothes, line up the filled clothes baskets on the laundry room counter, if you have one. If not, stack the baskets wherever it is convenient.

Create a mini-version of your box storage system. Design a smaller version of your box storage system to hold the clean clothes. If you decide to try this, use the boxes as laundry baskets, too.

Bring clean clothes to the individual bedrooms. If there is no room to store clothes in the laundry room, leave the baskets on each family member's bed for them to attend to when they arrive home.

Ironing Board and Iron

Try to keep an ironing board set up at all times. This makes spot ironing something that is much more likely to get done. Also, when clothes come out of the dryer, you can iron them while they are still damp. Doing so makes the job a little easier. (*Caution:* If you have little ones at home, keep the iron up and out of the way when not in use. It's not enough to unplug it and leave it on the board. A child can pull it down on her head.)

Keep your ironing board set up in your sewing room. If your laundry room is too small to accommodate your ironing board, see chapter fourteen on sewing rooms.

Purchase a hanging ironing board. Find one that will hang from the door, fold down for use, then fold back up. If neither of the options above is feasible, this can be an appealing solution.

Other Needs

• **Wastebasket.** For bits of paper, odds and ends, and lint, I just use an empty detergent box.

• **Container for change.** Each person who is old enough should empty his pockets before putting clothes into the laundry basket. Sometimes people forget, however, and you need something to contain money. A jelly jar or margarine tub will do. Leave the lid off. Mom (or whoever does the laundry) gets to keep the change.

• **Catch-all basket.** The same concept as the container for change. This one collects other pocket items that are missed: papers, whistles, frogs, and so forth. To discourage carelessness, you can keep these things in "jail" and charge "bail" to get them out.

• **Ink markers.** Particularly useful in a large family. I've heard of a woman who had six sons. Their jeans, underwear and socks all looked the same. The mother assigned each child a color and marked the clothing labels with that color for identification. She also purchased tube socks for each boy with stripes in the color they were assigned.

- **Lint brush.** Handy for catching lint before the item is put away.
- **Sponge or paper towels and spray cleaner.** For wiping down the machines, counter, shelves.
- **Items-to-buy list.** A sheet of paper taped inside a cabinet or tacked to the wall for keeping track of supplies as they get low. You'll need a pencil, too.

Now, go back through the items you've noted. You probably already have most of the necessary supplies around the house. As you gather them, keep track of the things you want to purchase on your need/want list. Organize the supplies you have on hand according to my instructions, and refer to the illustrations for ideas. Be sure to establish a specific home for each item, then label it!

Once you've organized your laundry room, your next step is to organize your laundry procedure.

ESTABLISHING A LAUNDRY PROCEDURE

These are suggestions to help you establish a solid routine for getting the laundry done. Since I've covered just about everything you could possibly want to do to a piece of laundry, you may not need to use every suggestion. Check off the ideas you like and want to incorporate.

By the way, in case you think I'm asking you to make too many decisions, let me remind you that once you've made them, you're done. As long as you follow your plan, you won't have to make these decisions again. You won't worry about when you'll get a chance to do laundry or what you're going to wear to work the next day. If you take a few minutes now to put your plans on paper, you will save yourself time and trouble in the future. Believe me, I know. I used to dread doing laundry. Now, it's no big deal.

Set aside a block of time. This means planning sufficient time for laundry and related tasks such as mending and ironing, if you intend to do it. If you have a helper, consider when that person will be available. Record your decision on your work schedule. To give you an example, I do laundry twice a week, on Monday and Thursday mornings. I usually do about three loads each day.

Choose specific days to wash specific items. Do this and you will always have what you need.

If you wash things randomly, you may wind up with three dozen clean bath towels but no clean underwear. If you make a conscious choice about this, you can plan loads that require less attention when you are busy with other things.

Monday morning is the major cleaning day for me. Thursday is my secondary cleaning day. For this reason, I wash items that do not require a lot of attention on Monday. For instance, on Mondays I wash sheets, towels and baby items. On Thursday, most things are still in pretty good shape from Monday's cleaning, so I can pay more attention to laundry. Therefore, on Thursday I wash work clothes, which usually require some ironing, casual clothes and underwear.

With this system, I have clothes for the following week prepared well in advance. I don't scurry around on Sunday night or Monday morning wondering how I can put an outfit together. Occasionally, I wash blankets, comforters, table linens, jackets, and so forth. I wash them when necessary, on my regular laundry days.

Choose an order for washing the clothes. For instance, wash white clothes first since they require hot water, which is usually limited. Also, dry clothes that require ironing when you can pay attention to removing them from the dryer quickly.

Make a decision about laundry pickup. Will you and your helper do it? Do you prefer that everyone bring their own to the laundry room on the appropriate day?

Have a plan for treating stains. For advice on presoaks, see the discussion earlier in this chapter.

Finishing touches. The clothes need to be sorted, folded or hung, and in some cases, ironed.

• When folding clothes, sort them into individual laundry baskets.

• If a garment needs to be ironed, plan to take it out of the dryer while still damp, and iron and hang it immediately.

• If you intend to iron at a later time, remember to schedule it. These procedures are covered earlier in this chapter.

Make a decision about clean clothes distribution. Choose one of these three options, and make it a routine:

- Put clean clothes away.
- Deposit baskets of clean clothes in individual rooms for the owner to put away.
- Leave baskets and hanging items in the laundry room for family members to pick up and put away.

If you follow my suggestions, your family will help you by doing the sorting, delivering and putting-away steps themselves.

PLANNING ON PAPER

A lot of organized people (myself included), believe that one of the important keys to staying organized is to put plans on paper. There's something about seeing plans in black and white that makes them more valid and concrete. This is an especially helpful practice when you are establishing or changing routine.

If you think it would help you to post a reminder of your laundry schedule, use the simple "Laundry Procedures" list on page 162.

IF IT LANDS IN JAIL, YOU PAY THE BAIL

A very time-consuming part of doing laundry is checking pockets. If you find that your family is lazy about it, you might want to give this a try.

First of all, family members who are old enough to take responsibility for cleaning out their pockets should certainly be doing so. Don't nag. Simply make sure that this is understood. Then, to discourage carelessness, keep anything you find in "jail." The owner has to pay "bail" to get it out. You can set the bail as you see fit, keeping in mind age and ability levels. For little ones, you may want to charge a hug, a kiss and a promise to try harder. For teens, you may delegate a small chore, take away a privilege or even charge a small cash fee. Obviously, you can't charge more than the item is worth. If all you ever find in their pockets are gum wrappers and other things to be thrown away, then call your charge a "sanitation" fee.

The idea is to teach family members to take proper responsibility and to be more considerate of you.

If you decide to try this, post a list of bail charges so that your children will know what their carelessness costs.

Make It Easy for Them to Cooperate

Just as it is helpful for you to get things down on paper, it helps other members of the family to have a clear understanding of rules, procedures and consequences. Keeping in mind all that you have learned, decide if you want to post a few lists and charts for your family. If so, which ones?

- laundry procedures
- bail charges
- laundry rules
- laundry how-tos
- helper chart

Use my samples below as a guideline for your ideas.

Laundry Procedures

On _____ (fill in the day of the week), I will wash these items in this order: _____, _____, _____. (Fill in types of clothing: underwear, sheets, towels, jeans and dark clothes, etc.)

On _____, I will wash these items in this order: _____, _____, _____.

On _____, I will wash these items in this order: _____, _____, _____.

Laundry Rules

- If it's on the floor, it won't get washed.
- If there's something in the pocket, it goes to jail.
- If a basket arrives unsorted, you pay maid service.
- Always check the lint filter before you dry.
- Clean the lint filter after each load.
- Wipe machines and tidy up when finished.
- When supplies are low, record them on the shopping list.

Laundry How-Tos

- If a basket arrives unsorted, sort it according to these categories: whites, colors, darks, towels, sheets, delicates.

- Check for stains. Treat stains using _____.
- Adjust the load size and water temperature on the washing machine.
  - Use (amount) of detergent.
  - Use (amount) of bleach, if necessary.
  - Use (amount) of fabric softener.
  - Dry items that wrinkle in small loads. Remove when still damp.
  - Hang up garments as they come from the dryer.
  - Fold other items and put into the correct basket.

What Your Helper Does

If you have a helper — a child who is learning about laundry procedures, or a spouse or roommate — you need to make their responsibilities clear, so your assistant will be able to successfully complete them. To help, post a simple chart such as the one shown on page 164.

Going to the Launderette

Careful planning is the key when you take your laundry out to be washed.

- Make sure you have enough laundry baskets.
- Do all sorting at home.
- Use pillowcases to transport items that you are not concerned about wrinkling, such as socks and undies.
- Dry items in small loads. (Costs the same.)
- Carry small containers of detergent and bleach.
- Separate everyone's clothes into individual baskets or boxes to bring laundry home in. (Saves time once at home again.)

Laundry Room Tips

- Make your work space as pleasant as possible. Paint the laundry room your favorite color.
- Limit your clothes! This is one of the biggest favors I have done for myself — less work, less washing, less mending and less money.
- Experiment with your schedule. If you have lots of laundry, consider doing one or two loads every day, rather than once or twice a week.
- Pin or tie drawstrings before washing.

- Pin buckles of overalls inside pockets to avoid clanking.
- Wash and dry lint-catching items inside out.
- Wash and dry lint-producing items smooth side out.
- Always clean the lint filter after every cycle.
- Use an aluminum venting hose on your dryer instead of plastic. (A fireman suggested this to me.)
- Do not dry items that wrinkle when you don't have time to remove them promptly. Dry them in small amounts to avoid tangling.
- If something does wrinkle, dry it again with a wet item.
- Remove items for ironing when they are still damp.

> ### What My Helper Does
> - Helps gather dirty clothes.
> - Helps sort.
> - Helps fold.
> - Helps hang.
> - Helps bring clean laundry to bedrooms.
> - Checks supplies. Records what's needed.
> - Cleans lint filter.
> - Wipes machines.

- Remove hanging items a few at a time, and let others continue to tumble dry.
- Hang all items in the same direction.
- When purchasing socks, buy several identical pairs. Your socks will always have a mate, even if one is lost.
- Socks that no longer have a mate can be used as dust mitts.
- To rid sweaters of pills, carefully "shave" them with a disposable razor.
- Never leave any appliance running when nobody is home.
- Separate the clothes that need to be dry cleaned and keep them in a special box or basket in your room.

CHAPTER FOURTEEN

SEWING AND CRAFTS

MAKING SURE YOU CAN FIND

YOUR NEEDLES IN THIS

ORGANIZATIONAL

HAYSTACK

*D*o you like to sew? Perhaps you enjoy crafts. Whatever the case, it's a wonderful creative outlet, and
getting this area organized makes it even more enjoyable. If you don't
have a whole room to dedicate to sewing and crafts (and who does?),
get your supplies well-organized and share space with another area.

These are a few suggestions about where to set up:

- Share space in an office, laundry room or guest room.
- Adapt a large closet.
- Use a portable table and store your supplies in your box storage
  system.

- As a last resort, use your bedroom.

As long as your supplies are well organized, you can set up your sewing machine just about anywhere. And, with all the organizing products available these days, it's probably easier than ever to get your creative side organized.

CHOOSING A MAIN STORAGE SYSTEM

Aside from having containers for organizing small supplies, you will need a central storage place. Rather than allowing zillions of small tools and supplies to scatter over every nearby surface, you can contain them in one location and get them as needed.

The type of central storage you use will depend on your circumstances. If you are fortunate enough to have a closet for this purpose, you could install shelves and create a version of the box storage system for sewing supplies. Another possibility is a basket storage system on open bookshelves, like the one used for toy storage. (See the illustration in chapter nine, on children's bedrooms.) Even an old chest of drawers could house your supplies. Think creatively, and remember that enclosed storage is better for reducing visual clutter. If all else fails, keep your individual supplies in small containers and contain them in two or three boxes in your box storage system.

Let's get started.

Step One: Designate the Purposes of the Sewing Room

The general purposes of the sewing room are:

☐ to sew new clothes
☐ to do repair work/mending
☐ to do crafts and other creative activities
☐ to teach children sewing skills

Step Two: Eliminate

Start by gathering your supplies and sorting them into groups of similar items:

☐ fabric   ☐ machine attachments
☐ patterns   ☐ books

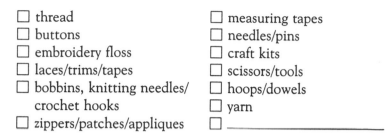

☐ thread   ☐ measuring tapes
☐ buttons   ☐ needles/pins
☐ embroidery floss   ☐ craft kits
☐ laces/trims/tapes   ☐ scissors/tools
☐ bobbins, knitting needles/   ☐ hoops/dowels
     crochet hooks   ☐ yarn
☐ zippers/patches/appliques   ☐ _____

As you go through each group, eliminate items that are worn, missing their pieces, out of style, broken, etc. There's no reasonable argument for keeping such things.

Step Three: Contain

Let's look at your supplies and easy ways to organize and contain them.

Fabric. Fabric should be separated by size. For instance, it's a good idea to separate large pieces used for sewing clothing from smaller pieces that will be used for crafts.

Then (especially if you have a lot of fabric), divide the larger pieces even further. Sort these by color or by fabric type, separating dressier fabrics from those that are more casual. By grouping fabrics this way, you'll have better knowledge of what is on hand and how much you have of a given type.

Next, roll the large pieces (do not fold—it can cause fading at the crease line) and secure them with a thin rubber band. If possible, stand the rolled fabric vertically in a box, so that you can easily view every piece that you have. If you lay the fabric down and stack it, you will have to dig to see what is available.

Another possibility is to ask your local fabric retailer for some of the cardboard forms that fabric comes on. Wrap your fabric around the forms and store them in a box or on a shelf. Small pieces and scraps should be kept in a container designated for crafts projects. No need to roll these.

If you are really a sewing nut and have tons of fabric, I suggest you catalog each piece. You will need a small filing box, such as a recipe box, and file cards. Staple a small swatch of fabric to a card and list information such as fabric type (e.g., cotton, wool, linen), the dimensions of the piece, and whether or not it has been pre-

Keep track of leftover fabrics by cataloging each piece on a 3" × 5" card.

shrunk. You should also include the pattern number that you origi-
nally intended to use. If you are in the habit of storing lots of fabric,
it's easy to forget what you bought it for.

Patterns. Patterns are one of the many things that seem to be
revered as sacred to the unorganized among the population. Why
anyone would save a pattern for a Nehru jacket or one missing half
its pieces, I do not know. (It would probably require thousands of
dollars and many years of therapy to find out.) At any rate, if you
have patterns of good quality, with all their pieces, that are still in
style, you can organize them in a couple of different ways:

• Use a small plastic basket and divide by age (child/teen/adult),
style (dressy/casual), and miscellaneous (costumes/crafts/house-
hold).
• Purchase pattern organizers at fabric stores.
• Make a pattern catalog by using a three-ring notebook and clear
plastic zip pockets (available at office supply stores). You can see the
patterns easily, and the pocket is roomier than the original envelope.
Separate the patterns by type, as suggested above.

Threads. There are different ways to organize threads. If you have
a large quantity of different types of thread, separate them first. For
instance, separate general purpose threads from machine embroidery
and hand-quilting threads. Then, group them by color. You have a
few choices for storage:

*Keep thread handy but out of the way. This wall-mounted board
with spindles for each spool of thread is ideal.*

• Use the spindles provided in the sewing machine cabinet. There probably won't be enough, so use these for basic colors. When you need to do mending, they will be handy.

• Use tiered spindles and store them in a container.

• Use a board with spindles and mount it on a nearby wall.

Buttons. If you have a hodgepodge of buttons in different sizes, shapes and colors, store them in any of the following ways:

• A clear plastic container such as a sherbet tub.

• Use a metal box with drawers (the kind often used in workshops) to keep separated by size, shape and colors. These units are also great for other small sewing items.

• To avoid losing a button that is part of a set, string the set on a large safety pin.

Embroidery floss. Floss can be separated by color or project.

Ziploc bags, the drawers of a metal box, and specially designed plastic containers are good storage options. (Floss boxes are available at fabric stores.)

Laces, trims, tapes. These accessories can be grouped by type and stored in clear plastic bags or the drawers of a metal box.

Bobbins. As with spools of thread, store basic colors in the sewing machine cabinet. If you need more space, use clear bobbin cases, which are available at fabric stores. Always keep your basic wardrobe colors stocked for mending.

Zippers, patches, appliques. These should be sorted and stored in clear plastic bags or the drawers of a metal box.

Machine attachments. Store your sewing machine accessories in the drawers of the sewing table, if they are used often enough to deserve a prime location. If not, store them in the drawers of a metal box, in a small basket or tray, or in your box storage system if you seldom use them.

KEEPING IT ALL TOGETHER

Once you have decided on a storage system — closet, box or basket — make the most of it. Not only can you store your various notions and supplies neatly, you can also store your ongoing projects.

Let's say you are working on three different projects at one time. You are sewing a tablecloth, knitting a sweater, and cross-stitching a sampler. Each project should be assigned to its own container, so that you can keep track of its pieces and patterns. Its also less likely to get damaged or tangled up with other work. When you are ready to proceed with a project, just grab your basket and go. It's very simple this way.

Tips

• Finish current and old projects before starting new ones. (If you no longer like it, throw it away, or give it to someone who will finish it.)

• Make the biblical concept your motto: Finishing is better than starting. Anyone can start a project, but a half-done project is useless. Become a finisher, and enjoy your efforts.

• Keep a basket of basic supplies handy. In it have the items you need each time you sew (scissors, measuring tape, seam ripper, pins, and so forth.)

• If you have room, post a bulletin board on the wall near your machine. Pin your pattern here. It keeps your hands free, and it's much easier than fighting that awkward paper.

• If you're in a cutting mode, pin and cut out all your current projects. Store each in its own box or basket, and work on it at your leisure.

• Tips on mending are covered in chapter thirteen.

CHAPTER FIFTEEN

THE OFFICE

NEVER FILE EVERYTHING UNDER

"MISCELLANEOUS" AGAIN

*M*ore than any other room of the home, the office can invoke feelings of panic and visions of mayhem. Many people find this area so confusing and frustrating that they simply ignore it, stacking and piling paperwork for years. The result is the worst of organizational nightmares. If you seem to be piled under by paperwork, take heart. Here's help.

TO FILE OR NOT TO FILE

It seems to me that the main concerns people have pertaining to paperwork are these:

1. What shall I keep? Will I *ever* need this? I better keep *everything*.
2. How in the world can I file it so that I can find it again?

My objectives for this chapter are to help you create an easy-to-use filing system for your necessary paperwork and to encourage you to eliminate your unnecessary paperwork.

Paper Training 101

I have found that files are much easier to manage if they are broken into relatively small groups. Consequently, my system is based on the concept of grouping files into several broad categories.

Most paperwork can be filed in these general categories: household, reference, fun, spouse, organizations, business and old. I like to use a different color of file for each category. It's fun and provides instant recognition. I prefer this system to alphabetizing, because it allows you to work with the fewest files possible. This helps keep you from getting overwhelmed.

Another reason I do not recommend alphabetizing is that choosing an appropriate heading can drive you crazy: "Let's see, should I call this file *Vitamin C* or *Health* or *Nutrition* or *Fitness* or *Cold Cures?*" In fact, I think my system is about as easy as you can get and still stay organized.

One important aspect of my method is the use of a "handling" system to process the paperwork. The handling system is the foundation, and it is a wonderful way to simplify and demystify the filing process.

To help you understand the system, I will take you through a mock office hours session. You will be able to see exactly how I handle each piece of paper. As always, take things one step at a time. If you have a lot of paperwork accumulated, don't expect to get through it in one afternoon. The more paperwork you have (and the more you insist on keeping), the longer this job will take. Try to make the best of it. It's a very important area to get under control.

Step One: Designate the Purposes of the Office

Normally, you will need your office to be equipped for the following purposes:

☐ pay bills
☐ store paperwork
☐ write letters
☐ make telephone calls
☐ reconcile checks
☐ plan personal time, make to do list
☐ _____
☐ _____

If you do not already have an office, decide where to set up based on your list above. For instance, if you want to be able to make telephone calls, you need to set up near a telephone jack or have the phone company install an extension jack in an area you would otherwise not consider. (This can be done at a fairly reasonable price.) An alternative is to invest in a cordless phone.

If you need to share your office, a guest room or sewing room is a good candidate. Wherever you choose, it's important that it feels comfortable, so you'll use it. Here's a lesson I learned.

In one of our homes, I set up my office in a loft room that had a built-in desk. It seemed to be the logical place for an office. The room was light and airy, with lots of windows. I thought it had great atmosphere. In went the computer, files and so forth. A problem quickly surfaced. When I was doing my office work, I felt like I was a million miles away from my family. I felt lonely and isolated.

I wound up developing a portable office system that I set up on my dining room table (when necessary) so that I could be closer to my loved ones. I liked it so much, I still use that basic system to this day. So much for a fancy shmancy office. Of course, there's the distinct possibility that you may cherish a couple of hours of quiet time, even if it means paying bills. The point is, make things as comfortable as possible in your situation.

Step Two: Eliminate

Now that you have designated your office purposes and assigned it a space, it's time to start dealing with the paper.

Gather your bills, letters, insurance policies, wills and medical information. Don't forget to look under the couch cushions, behind the microwave, and between the fridge and the counter. Collect everything you can possibly find and bring it to your office area.

If you already have files, your job will be somewhat easier. You may be able to skip the gathering stage and move on to the sorting phase.

Sorting Your Paperwork Into Workable Piles

Depending on the degree of disarray, you may feel overwhelmed when you gather your paperwork and see the amount you have accumulated. Perhaps this will motivate you to get rid of some of it.

If you have quite a bit of paperwork, sort it into large containers. Gather some baskets or boxes from your box storage system. Label each container with these categories:

Household. I call this the "household working file." These are the files that deal with your home, finances, bill paying and everyday life. This is the most important file system you will have.

Fun. This is for paperwork on any subject that you consider fun — dream house ideas, party plans, creative writing ideas, holiday ideas, recipes.

Reference/Information. This is for how-to information, health tips, mail-order information and catalogs, appliance manuals, computer information, maps and any similar material that you would like to keep.

Business. If you operate a business out of your home, you will need to have a special system for business-related paperwork.

Organizations. Keep a file for paperwork related to the various organizations — clubs, church, political groups, homeowner's association, etc. — that you are affiliated with.

Old. This is also called the "dead" file by many people. These are important papers that you never or rarely need. They can be kept out of your main filing systems and out of your way. One example is your marriage certificate. Perhaps you want to keep it for sentimental reasons, but have you ever been asked to produce it? This category is also for old tax returns (going back seven years), canceled checks (older than this year), and receipts you are saving in case your taxes are audited. By simply designating much of your paperwork to this category, you can remove it from your regular filing system, uncluttering it and making things easier on yourself.

Spouse. This is a filing system for paperwork belonging to your spouse.

Unless you have mountains of unusual paperwork, you should be able to file your papers using these main categories.

By the way, you may not have paperwork related to every one of these general categories. Good for you! Don't imagine that there is something wrong if you don't. These are very broad categories, suitable for dividing paper into workable piles. Later, you will break these down into more specific categories and make individual hanging files for them.

As you create and organize your files, there will be paperwork that you can eliminate entirely. If you are not sure if you can live without it, ask yourself two questions:

1. **Is it truly irreplaceable?** Much of the paperwork that people save can be replaced, *if necessary*. This is particularly true of reference information, how-to materials and so forth. But even if an item is irreplaceable, you need to decide if it is still of importance in your life. If you are still saving valentines from your fifth-grade sweetheart, it may be time to let go.

2. **What would happen if I did throw it away?**
   a. I would be arrested.
   b. I would wrinkle before my time.
   c. I would feel a giddy, wonderful sense of relief.

If your answer is "c," then *toss it!* If not, make a file.

New This Fall — Nehru Jackets

Most people who have a problem with clutter in other areas of their lives have it in their files as well. Clutter in the form of unnecessary paperwork bogs down a filing system and, consequently, its effectiveness.

Generally speaking, there are two categories of paperwork: papers that are necessary for responsible people to save, and those that are optional. It's important to know the distinction. The necessary paperwork, we have no control over. We must have it, so we must have a system for retrieving it. Optional paperwork is another story entirely. In my experience, most of this optional paperwork is being saved for "someday" (that magical day no one has yet to know) and most of it is unnecessary, because it is informative or instructive and can easily be replaced if someday ever does come.

The problem with informative paperwork is that it is usually dated. I've had clients who saved informative paperwork for decades. What good are medical tips that are thirty years old? Personally, I prefer to confer with my doctor on the most current treatments available. And how about beauty tips and hairstyles that old? We'd look pretty silly sporting that look today.

If this sounds all too familiar to you, do yourself a favor. Let go. Your local public library is a fountain of information. Thanks to your library, you can get your hands on information about any subject you desire without having to pay for or store it. When you're finished, return it to them and let them worry about finding a place for it. Believe me, they're better equipped.

Since most of us have large enough piles that are worth saving, it's very important to eliminate as much of the optional paperwork as you have the courage to do. And, if for some reason you must have fashion and beauty tips that are thirty years old, your library could no doubt get them for you.

Step Three: Contain

Once you've set out on the great paper chase, equip yourself with some basic tools. The things you need to set up my system are as follows:

- Hanging file folders — fifty to seventy-five to start, more if you anticipate the need. I also recommend using a variety of colors.
- File tabs and inserts — should come with files.
- Manila folders — at least ten.
- *Place* to hang your files — filing cabinet, filing drawer in a desk or filing boxes.
- Bulletin board, pushpins.
- Calendar with squares large enough for notations.
- Pens.

By the way, it sometimes takes experimentation to determine which type of file storage system you will be most comfortable with. When I was a newlywed setting up my office, I went right out and purchased a two-drawer file cabinet. After all, that's how files are supposed to be kept, isn't it? I later decided that the file drawers were cumbersome, so I sold the cabinet and my desk and purchased a desk with a file drawer. Then I discovered that this wasn't as wonderful as I had hoped. Later, in conjunction with a move to the house I mentioned earlier, I switched to a portable cardboard box system.

Now, some of you may think that's a lot of bother to go through and, in some respects, that's true. But since the resale value of office furniture is so high, it didn't cost me much, and I discovered a system I preferred to any other. To me, it was worth the extra effort.

If you want to use a portable system, purchase cardboard file boxes at an office supply store. Look for the type that holds legal-size files one way, and letter-size the other.

Office Supplies

The following is a list of other office-related accessories. It's probably a good idea to have all of these items, and you may have them around the house already. Keep your want/need list handy for anything else you think of.

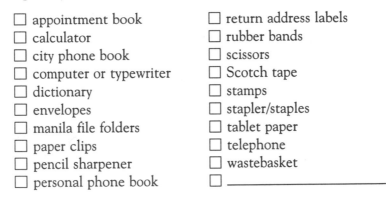

- ☐ appointment book
- ☐ calculator
- ☐ city phone book
- ☐ computer or typewriter
- ☐ dictionary
- ☐ envelopes
- ☐ manila file folders
- ☐ paper clips
- ☐ pencil sharpener
- ☐ personal phone book

- ☐ return address labels
- ☐ rubber bands
- ☐ scissors
- ☐ Scotch tape
- ☐ stamps
- ☐ stapler/staples
- ☐ tablet paper
- ☐ telephone
- ☐ wastebasket
- ☐ _____

Tips for Setting Up Files

Before you begin to actually put your paperwork into files, here are some tips to help prepare for the process:

• Use a dark felt-tip pen to label your files and an easy-to-read, block-letter style of printing.

• When making files, stagger the tabs so that you can easily see all the files in the system. Some people prefer to affix the tabs to the front of the file, rather than the rear. Do what seems most comfortable for you.

• If you anticipate a problem misplacing files, use a folder to hold the contents of each hanging file, and remove only that when retrieving paperwork. That way, the hanging file never has to leave its spot in the lineup.

• A typical hanging file can easily accommodate twenty-five pieces of paper. Don't try to cram in 457. Make another file.

SETTING UP YOUR BASIC HOUSEHOLD FILE

Your first step in organizing your papers into files is to set up your household file system with the papers you've gathered into your household/working box. So, at this time, gather your hanging files, tabs, manilla folders, pens and household box.

Next, create the five hanging files that constitute the handling system. These will help tremendously as you sort your paperwork and mail as it comes into your home.

Mail. This is basically a holding tank for your mail until you have time to sort it into the handling system.

To do. This is your file of things to do or take care of during your office hours session each week. These to do things are the actions you take in response to the mail you received that week.

Financial. This is the holding file that contains the bills you have received and will be paying that week.

Spouse. This is where you file items that are addressed to or pertain to your spouse.

To file. Another holding area. Keep items in here that you will file during your office hours session for that week.

I suggest you also create a file for your file tabs and inserts at this time. Keep it directly behind the other five files.

Mail and other paperwork that comes into your house can be sorted into one of these files. This helps tremendously, particularly if you have a difficult time trying to make sense of your paperwork. By breaking things into manageable bites, you have a better chance of becoming, and then staying, organized.

Let's continue, and decide on the other files we want for our household system.

Pending. This is the file for items that you are waiting for a response to.

Banking. You may want to have a separate file for each of your accounts — savings, checking, CDs, loans. This is where you keep your savings passbook, checking deposit receipts and canceled checks. Manila folders can separate the groups for you, within one hanging file.

Utilities. If you like to keep receipts and information on your utilities, create a file for gas, electric, phone, and so forth. After these bills have been taken out of the financial folder and paid, file the stubs or receipts here. Or, if you like to save them for only a few months, keep one main utilities file and put individual utility receipts in manila folders. That is what I do.

Medical. This file contains blank insurance forms, bill receipts, explanation of benefits, etc. I suggest having a file for each member of the family, but individual folders within a hanging file might work well for you.

Dental. Same as medical.

Insurance. Home, car, life, and so forth. You have a few different choices here. One is to have a separate file for each and keep a copy of the policy in the file. Keep receipts of payment and settlement papers. You may also want to keep a note about your agent — name, address and phone number.

The second option is to keep insurance information within the file on the item that's insured. For instance, we had a Honda Accord, so we had a Honda file. In it we kept *everything* pertaining to that car: the insurance policy, a copy of the title, payment stubs, receipts for repairs, etc. This is probably the easiest way, because it reduces your number of files and makes it easy to find needed items.

A third option is to have one main file for all your insurance. Use folders to separate them by category.

Children. You may want to have a file for each member of the family, keeping information that pertains to them in one place.

Taxes. This is for your most current tax return, tax deductible receipts, canceled checks for deductible items, etc. Keep your accountant's name, address and number here, as well as the number for the IRS question and answer line.

Credit cards. This is a file to house receipts for each of your credit cards. Manila folders can separate Visa from MasterCard, and so forth. As the bills arrive, they go into the financial folder to await payment. At that time, you can compare purchase receipts with bills and make a quick check for inaccuracies. Your bill stub and the receipts, if you care to save them longer, can now stay in the individual folders.

Check stubs. If you save stubs from paychecks, create a file for them.

Receipts. A place to keep receipts for the miscellaneous items you buy. You may want to return an item, or you may need proof of purchase if the item breaks. A main file makes it easy to find a receipt if you need it.

Home improvements. This is a file for keeping track of improvements you have done. If you prefer, you could keep this in its own folder in your tax file.

Estate. This should include a copy of your will, information about your assets, and other material needed in the event of your death.

Household inventory. Ideally, you should have pictures or a video tape of your belongings in a safe deposit box. Keep photos and a written record of belongings here.

Note: Your important papers should be copied, and the originals kept in a safe deposit box.

In summary, the files that will hang in your household system include any items that pertain to your daily life and your current important papers.

SETTING UP THE OTHER SYSTEMS
Let's move on to the other file categories.

Reference/Information
Choose a file color you like and get your hanging files, tabs, folders, pen, and your information box and begin to make files according to the categories you have. Use broad terms.

For instance, you might have a hanging file labeled "Health." In this broad file category, put your information on all aspects of health — tips, exercises, vitamin information, the latest news on a particular disease, news on cures, etc. Unless you have tremendous amounts of paperwork (in which case you need to do some serious eliminating), there is no need to make individual files or folders for each segment. Remember, we are trying to keep as simple as possible an area of our lives that can be very confusing. This is why I urge you not to over organize. You'll just drive yourself crazy if you get too picayune.

In the reference/information file system, you may also have files for:

- Maps/local.
- Maps/out-of-state.
- How-to information.
- Information/warranties on appliances that stay with the house if you move. (I keep a notebook with this information and keep it handy to refer to. When I move, I leave it for the new owners.)
- Information/warranties on items that go with you if you move.
- Things to do locally. This is a fun file to keep for ideas on local attractions and entertainment if you have out-of-town visitors or if you have extra time yourself.
- Information on colleges. If you have a son or daughter applying to college, gather the information here unless they want to keep it in their own filing system.

Continue in this manner, making broad files for all your information and eliminating what you can until your box is empty.

Organizations

Next, work from your organizations box. Choose a color and get your supplies. You may want to create files for:

- church
- women's club
- political
- volunteer
- charities
- Boy Scouts
- sorority
- Brownies
- homeowners' association
- alumni association
- craft club

Create a file for any organization you belong to and have paper-work for. Some of these can be grouped. For instance, if you are associated with several charities, doing fund raising and volunteer work, you can have one main charities file, then use folders within it to separate your paperwork on each charity.

If you belong to only one or two organizations, you probably won't want to create a system for those. Let's say you belong to a craft club and you are a den mother for your child's club. You can place those two files in your fun system. If the only organization you belong to is the homeowners' association from your subdivision, you can keep that file in your household system.

Fun

Next, set up your fun file. As with the others, you will need your supplies. Some of the files you may want are:

- dream house
- gift ideas
- party ideas
- fun cooking
- crafts
- gardening
- concepts
- holidays
- hobbies to try

Again, use broad categories. For instance, in your dream house file you may have professional house plans, ideas you have sketched, articles on how to lay out an efficient kitchen or bathroom, decorating ideas or color scheme palettes—anything and everything that pertains to your dream house. Don't try to make files for each little category or you will drive yourself nuts! Eliminate as much as you can. If you've got brochures on seventeen styles of kitchen cabinets, you can certainly eliminate at least twelve of them.

Spouse

The spouse file is, naturally, best set up by that person. Since you are now the organization expert in the family, you can offer help. If your spouse says it's OK, go ahead and set up the files. If your spouse does not want to set up a filing system or have you do it either, then store the spouse's box of papers in the box storage system until they are ready.

Here are some sample files for this category:

- military service papers
- sentimental papers
- college information
- letters
- occupational papers
- hobby pamphlets/instructions

Old

To set up your old system, gather your necessary tools and your box of old papers. Try to eliminate as much as you can here. Your files might include:

- tax returns
- real estate closings
- canceled checks
- love letters
- receipts for audits
- high school diploma
- marriage certificate
- sentimental papers
- adoption papers

Use this system for any papers that you want to save, but that would be in your way in your main file. Think of this file as a box storage system for your paperwork.

Business

If you operate a business from your home, prepare that filing system next. Gather your files, tabs, folders, pen and box of paperwork and continue in the same manner. Store anything and everything that relates to the business. Let's look at some of the files you may want to include:

- license
- vendor list

- accounts payable/rent
- accounts receivable
- utility bills
- client list/contacts
- gasoline/mileage
- advertising
- other expenses

If you run a business from your home, it's probably a good idea to get help from your accountant about what is appropriate to keep and what can be discarded. Another source of help is the Small Business Administration. If you live near a major college, they may have a small business development project that can offer you advice.

MAKING IT WORK

Having your paperwork in neat little hanging files is not all there is to successful paperwork management. Other components are necessary to make this system work for you. Once you've got your files set up, you need to make some decisions about how you will keep them up. You need to schedule an office hours session in your permanent weekly schedule. At first, until you get comfortable with the system, plan to spend one to one-and-a-half hours a week on this session. Use the time to pay bills, write letters, make phone calls, balance your checkbook, and so forth.

In addition to scheduling office hours, make a decision on how to handle mail and other paperwork that comes into your life and home on a daily basis. If several people in your house receive mail, decide on a pick-up spot for them to collect it. Either deliver the mail to their individual rooms or designate a place where they can pick it up every day.

After you separate your mail and your spouse's from the children's and the household mail, take yours and your spouse's immediately to your office area. Absolutely resist the temptation to dive into it before you get to the office. The only exception to this rule might be a magazine that you stop to put in the magazine rack next to your favorite reading chair. Do not stop to read it at this time.

It is so important for you to resist opening the mail at any spot other than your office area, because that is precisely how the paper trail begins and gets out of hand. If you *do* open it as you walk through the house, you may wind up with an electric bill in the kitchen, a letter from your friend on your dresser, your new insurance policy on top of the washing machine, etc. Do yourself a favor — *take it to the office!*

THE MAIL BAG — PROCESSING MAIL THROUGH THE SYSTEM

Let's go through our sample mail bag. I have collected my mail, and this is what I have:

- Visa card bill
- fabric store sale notice
- canceled checks from bank
- electric bill
- letter to my husband
- solicitation from charity
- notice from pediatrician
- update from Congress
- personal letter
- community theater schedule

I have ten pieces of mail that I bring to the office. Since tomorrow is my office hours day, I decide to process the mail through the handling system. All ten pieces of mail will be dealt with at this time. I have three choices: I can throw it away, take action on it now (I won't, because I will save it for tomorrow's office session), or I can file it to act on it later (that's what I will do).

All of this mail will go through a quick decision-making process. Let's go through each piece in the order listed above.

1. Visa card bill — financial
2. fabric store sale notice — trash
3. canceled checks from bank — to do
4. electric bill — financial
5. letter to my husband — spouse
6. solicitation from charity — financial
7. notice from pediatrician — to do
8. update from Congress — to do

9. personal letter — to do
10. community theater schedule — file

I am now through for the day. The whole process took less than two minutes; maybe five if I stopped to read the letter.

OFFICE HOURS SESSION

It is now the day and time for my office hours session. I have allotted one hour in my weekly schedule. It's probably best if you can do this with your spouse, but that seems to be a rarity in most families.

The first thing I do is go through my To Do file and take care of the items in it. I have four things.

1. canceled checks
2. notice from pediatrician
3. personal letter
4. update from Congress

Though I expect to have enough time to take care of all of these things, I make a mental priority list. You never know what may come up to interrupt you.

1. My son is the first priority. I have received notice from his pediatrician that there is a new vaccination being given, and would I please call for an appointment. I call, make the appointment, mark the day and time on my monthly calendar, and make a note of it in my appointment book. I throw away the notice.

2. Next, the update from my congressperson has upsetting news. I want to respond. I expect a reply to my letter, so I write it on the computer and make two copies — one I send and the other I keep. I make a notation on my calendar for a date six weeks from today, a fair amount of time to allot for a response. If I have not had a response by that day, I will decide how to pursue the matter. I put the letter from my congressperson along with the letter I have written into my To File file.

3. I reconcile my canceled checks and put them in the To File hanging file folder.

4. I decide not to write to my friend at this time; I will write to her later in the evening. I make a note on my to do list for the day and put her letter in my writing basket.

That takes care of all the items in my To Do file. Now, let's see what I have in my Financial file.

1. Visa card bill
2. electric bill
3. solicitation from charity

1. Visa bill. I go to my Visa file and remove the receipts for my most recent purchases. A quick review tells me everything is in order. If there had been a discrepancy, I would have called the customer service number on the bill to take care of it immediately. I write the check, stamp the envelope, and set the bill aside to mail. I put the receipts in an envelope marked with the month, and put the envelope and bill stub into my To File file.

2. Electric bill. I open the electric bill, write a check, stamp the envelope, put on my return address, and set it aside to mail. On the bill stub, I note the date and amount paid and the check number. I put the bill stub in the To File folder.

3. Charity solicitation. I support the charity that sent this solicitation and am able to send a contribution at this time. I note on the check that this is a tax deductible item. Next month, when I reconcile the checks, I will remove that one and insert it into the tax deductibles file. I throw away the letter. (If I could not afford a donation at this time, I would have thrown the letter away. You can no doubt donate at any time without the letter, and there will most likely be another solicitation soon, anyway.)

That concludes the Financial file. Next, I work from the To File file. I have several items in this file.

1. theater schedule
2. update from Congress and my response
3. canceled checks
4. Visa stub/receipts
5. electric stub

Now let's disperse these items into my system in this order:

1. Theater schedule. When I received the theater schedule in the mail, I knew it was something I would be interested in. I do not want to commit to season tickets at this time, so I will file it for later

reference. Since this is the first time I have received a theater schedule, I do not have an existing file. I do not want to create a file for this subject only. Instead, I'll file it in a broad category such as Entertainment and file it in my Fun system.

2. Update from Congress/my letter to Congress. Normally, I would have read the letter from my congressperson and then thrown it away. Since I chose to write a letter and am expecting a response, I will keep these in my Pending file. I have already put a reminder on my calendar to take action if I do not receive a response by a certain date. I marked the reminder on the same day of the week as my office hours session, so I won't miss it.

3. The canceled checks go in my Banking file in my canceled checks folder.

4. Visa stubs and receipts are kept in my Charge Cards file in my Visa folder.

5. The electric bill stub is put in my Utilities file in my Electricity folder.

That takes care of my To File paperwork. The only thing I have left at this point is the Spouse file, which my husband, Steve, will take care of himself.

That ends my weekly office hours session. I will not go through this again for a week. The things I will do are collect the mail, store it in the Mail file, or sort it into the handling system.

Though it may take you a while to get your files set up, once your system is established, it's a breeze to keep maintained. Don't panic. Good luck!

THE END

Well, if you're reading this, you must be finished. (If not, quit cheating and get back to organizing, nosey!) If you're still reading, I guess it's safe to assume you have succeeded in your mission. You have gone from killing time to investing it, from being a slave to clutter to being clutter free and proud of it. You've purged your cabinets, closets and drawers of junk and corralled and contained their contents. You've learned to delegate jobs and get cooperation from your family. You've stopped piling up your paperwork and are now an expert filer. You know exactly where your car keys are, what you're having for dinner a week from Thursday, and how to locate your tax return of four years ago. As they say, you've come a long way, baby. I'm proud of you.

You've done the hard work. Now, you've just got to maintain it with your new habits. Keep up with your weekly work schedule, keep on top of clutter, and give that box storage system a workout. Make runs to your favorite charity with donations a couple of times a year, and keep steadfast in your efforts to resist unneeded purchases. If you feel yourself slackening, refer back to your "before" pictures; that should get you back on track.

I want you to know that I have thoroughly enjoyed writing this book for you, and my sincerest wish is that it helps you make a profound lifestyle change. You know, I call this the end, but it's really just the beginning. Now, you can really start to enjoy your life, pursue your goals and dreams, and contribute to making this world a better place.

I wish you all good things, and most of all, a fulfilling, productive and orderly life. God bless.

Pam

INDEX

Other Books of Interest

Home/Family
  The Christmas Lover's Handbook, $14.95
  Clutter's Last Stand, $10.95
  The Complete Guide to Recycling at Home: How to Take Responsibility, Save Money, and Protect the Environment, $14.95
  Confessions of a Happily Organized Family, $10.95
  Conquering the Paper Pile-Up, $11.95
  The Greatest Gift Guide Ever, 2nd Edition, $8.95
  How to Conquer Clutter, $10.95
  How to Get Organized When You Don't Have the Time, $10.95
  How to Have a Big Wedding on a Small Budget, $12.95
  The Big Wedding on a Small Budget Planner & Organizer, $12.95
  How to Have a Fabulous, Romantic Honeymoon on a Budget, $12.95
  Into the Mouths of Babes: A Natural Foods Cookbook for Infants and Toddlers, $6.95
  Is There Life After Housework?, $10.95
  It Doesn't Grow on Trees, $2.95
  It's Here . . . Somewhere, $10.95
  Make Your House Do the Housework, $12.95
  The Melting Pot Book of Baby Names, 2nd Ed., $8.95
  A Parent's Guide to Teaching Music, $7.95
  A Parent's Guide to Band and Orchestra, $7.95
  A Parent's Guide to Teaching Art: How to Encourage Your Child's Artistic Talent and Ability, $5.95
  Raising Happy Kids on a Reasonable Budget, $10.95
  Slow Down . . . And Get More Done, $11.95
  Step-by-Step Parenting, Revised & Updated, $9.95
  Streamlining Your Life, $11.95
  Unpuzzling Your Past: A Basic Guide to Genealogy, 2nd Ed., $11.95
Finance
  Becoming Financially Sound in an Unsound World, $14.95
  Cleaning Up for a Living: Everything You Need to Know to Become a Successful Building Service Contractor (2nd Ed.), $12.95
  College Funding Made Easy: How to Save for College While Maintaining Eligibility for Financial Aid, $12.95
  The Complete Guide to Buying and Selling Real Estate, $9.95
  The Complete Guide to Buying Your First Home, $14.95
  Homemade Money: The Definitive Guide to Success in a Homebased Business, $18.95
  How to Sell Your Home When Homes Aren't Selling, $16.95
  How to Succeed as a Real Estate Salesperson: A Comprehensive Training Guide, $14.95
  Legal Aspects of Buying, Owning, and Selling a Home, $12.95
  Little People: Big Business: A Guide to Successful In-Home Day Care, $7.95
  Rehab Your Way to Riches: Guide to High Profit/Low Risk Renovation of Residential Property, $14.95
  Single Person's Guide to Buying a Home: Why to Do It and How to Do It, $14.95
  The Student Loan Handbook: All About the Stafford Loan Program and Other Forms of Financial Aid, 2nd Ed., $7.95
  Success, Common Sense and the Small Business, $11.95

Hobbies

Breeding and Showing Purebred Dogs: More Adventures on the Road To Westminster, $7.95

Collecting Coins for Pleasure and Profit, $18.95

Collecting Stamps for Pleasure & Profit, $8.95

The Crafts Supply Sourcebook: A Comprehensive Shop-by-Mail Guide, 2nd Ed., $14.95

Fabulous Play House Plans, $16.95

Making "Movies" Without a Camera: Inexpensive Fun with Flip Books and Other Animation Gadgets, $7.95

Secrets of Buying Art: Photography, $16.95

For a complete catalog of Betterway Books write to the address below. To order, send a check or money order for the price of the book(s). Include $3.00 postage and handling for 1 book, and $1.00 for each additional book. Allow 30 days for delivery.

Betterway Books
1507 Dana Avenue, Cincinnati, Ohio 45207
Credit card orders call TOLL-FREE
1-800-289-0963
Quantities are limited; prices subject to change without notice.